I0579905

CULINARY VIETNAM

CULINARY VIETNAM

DANIEL HOYER

GIBBS SMITH
TO ENRICH AND INSPIRE HUMANKIND

Salt Lake City | Charleston | Santa Fe | Santa Barbara

First Edition
1 2 3 4 5   09 10 11 12 13

Text © 2009 Daniel Hoyer
Location Photography © 2009 Aidan Dockery
Food Photography © 2009 Marty Snortum

Published by
Gibbs Smith
P.O. Box 667
Layton, Utah 84041

Orders: 1.800.835.4993
www.gibbs-smith.com

Designed by Debra McQuiston
Printed and bound in China
Gibbs Smith books are printed on either recycled,
100% post-consumer waste, FSC-certified papers or
on paper produced from a 100% certified sustainable
forest/controlled wood source.

Library of Congress Cataloging-in-Publication Data

Hoyer, Daniel.
Culinary Vietnam / Daniel Hoyer ; photographs by
Aidan Dockery and Marty Snortum. — 1st ed.
p. cm.
ISBN-13: 978-1-4236-0320-7
ISBN-10: 1-4236-0320-6
1. Cookery, Vietnamese. I. Title.
TX724.5.V5H693 2009
641.59597—dc22
2008054226

For you again, Ian: your spirit lingers
and continues to guide me. Our journey together has been bittersweet
but it always follows the path with a
heart. Peace.

ACKNOWLEDGMENTS

I owe much thanks to many for this book. For some of you, I do not even know your names, but I am grateful for your help. Those that have especially helped, guided or inspired me include: Pepe, Marny, Phuong, Hue, Tra My, Huy, Ha, Aidan, Moon (Hang), Tung, Marty, and Khai. Nancy and Tristan, thank you for your willingness to try new things and your patience for my harebrained schemes. Tram, thank you for all of your thoughtful insight into the philosophy and practice of food in your amazing country, I am fortunate to have a "niece" like you. Finally, Lai, I do not think you know how much help you have been to me. You opened many doors to Vietnam that I would not have found so easily myself and taught me much about the "Vietnamese way." I am eternally grateful.

Today's Vietnamese cooking has been informed and shaped into its unique identity through its history, climate, and geography and, perhaps more than anything else, by the tenacious, resourceful, creative, clever, and gracious people of that country.

PREFACE

Along with many of my friends, both American and Vietnamese, you may wonder why I have chosen to write about Vietnamese cooking. The other common question is, "How do you, as a foreigner, have the background, experience, and expertise to try to teach others about this cuisine that has been developing for thousands of years?"

The first one is easy. Vietnam has been beckoning me for many years, starting during the war years, when I was faced with the prospect of being drafted and had watched friends, classmates, relatives, and neighbors who were affected by the war, either by serving or through the clash of ideology that caused so much divisiveness in our country. I received a personal reprieve and was spared a difficult decision when President Nixon cancelled the draft in July of 1973, but not before the war had stamped an indelible impression on me. I lost friends through battle casualties and because of disagreements over the conflict. Our nation is still reeling from that era, and feelings remain deep and intense. In the late '70s and early '80s, there was an influx of Vietnamese refugees arriving in the United States, and many of them found work in the restaurant industry or opened places of their own. I had the pleasure of working with some of these amazing people during my restaurant career, and the Vietnamese restaurants that began springing up provided my first taste of what has become one of my favorite foods. Interestingly, some of my new Vietnamese friends and coworkers actually taught me how to cook Chinese food, since many hailed from the Saigon area and had worked for Chinese restaurants or were ethnic Chinese themselves. I applied this newfound knowledge a few years later when I opened a critically acclaimed Chinese restaurant in a ski resort in Colorado—no mean feat for a boy from Kansas.

I continued to be aware of Vietnam and the difficult times the people there were facing during the '80s and early '90s, and I noted the positive changes that were taking place in economic development and personal freedoms as the '90s progressed. During that time, I made a very close friend who was of Vietnamese and French descent. His father's family had evacuated to France after the collapse of the colonial system, and he was born in France. His father had since returned to his home country, first for some humanitarian work and then to live there again. My friend visited his father in Saigon around 1995, shortly after the country was opened again to Westerners, and then returned to live there for some time. He shared many stories with me and rekindled my interest in Vietnamese food and culture. He also insisted that I needed to visit, as he felt that the cooking there was something that I could relate to and that I would find it a fascinating place. We talked a lot about the possibility of starting some culinary tours there, similar to what I was developing in Mexico. For some reason, we were never able to coordinate our schedules or budgets, and we were unable to travel to Vietnam together.

All of this—along with an emerging Vietnamese restaurant scene, the availability of previously hard-to-find ingredients, and an increasing interest in Asian flavors in America and Europe—fueled my interest in Vietnamese cooking and the possibility of visiting and writing about the country.

As to my credentials for writing a cookbook about Vietnam, I have nothing but a powerful interest and curiosity, a sympathetic view, and experience in writing about another country's cuisine from a nonnative perspective, namely Mexico. In *Culinary Mexico*, I approached the cooking of that country as an informed outsider who had immense respect for the culture and cooking. In it, I attempted to help illuminate the history, cultural background, traditions, and techniques of the cuisine for the non-Mexican reader. I will let the results speak for themselves; however, one reaction to that effort makes me very proud. Many Mexicans have told me that they recognize some of their favorite dishes and appreciate the accuracy and respect that I have given to the cooking of their native country. They also tell me that they have learned some new

aspects to Mexican cooking, as I tried to cover the entire scope of the cuisine, and that there was information available about other regions' approaches to cooking that they had never understood before. I do not claim to be an expert on all things pertaining to Mexican cooking; I only wanted to give a point of view and to help with preserving some of the traditions and connect them with the contemporary developments in Mexican food. I have the same goals with *Culinary Vietnam.*

There is no possibility that I can cover all aspects of Vietnamese cooking, which would be a daunting, near-impossible task even for a native-born Vietnamese cook. The cuisine has a history of thousands of years in development and countless influences from other cultures, as well as regional and personal variations too numerous to catalog. I am not attempting to write the definitive collection of Vietnamese recipes; what I hope to do is to open a window into the methods, theories, and background of the cuisine and to give some historical and cultural context to it all while showing the reader just how broad the scope of Vietnamese cooking is. My target readers are Western cooks, but my hope is that Vietnamese cooks will also find it accurate, interesting, and informative. I have used all of the resources that I had available: several visits to the country, where I observed, experienced, and took in as much about the food and culture as I could; cookbooks; magazines; restaurants; markets; advice, instruction, and recipes from Vietnamese friends and acquaintances; the Internet; and countless hours of experimenting and practicing in my own kitchen. The recipes herein are unavoidably colored and informed by my own cultural background, experiences, cooking style, and tastes; however, at all times I have tried to honor the soul of Vietnamese cooking and to give an accurate portrayal of the cuisine of that country. In some cases, I have changed ingredients to suit my tastes, the tastes of Western cooks, and the availability of ingredients in the West. I have tried to remain true to the premise or essence of the dishes though. My goal is to inspire cooks everywhere to cook more Vietnamese dishes and to help them along on a journey of learning and enjoying the wonderful food of this amazing country.

INTRODUCTION

Vietnam is a country that has a long and colorful history. It was first populated by a variety of indigenous groups, many who are still evident today. The Chinese were early invaders and had a lasting influence on the cooking and culture of the country. From India came the Buddhist philosophy that was integrated with many of the animist beliefs that were widely held. Vietnam has a long and storied royal lineage and was later colonized by the French. Revolutions followed, and the recent war with the U.S. and the unification of the country in 1975 all had a profound effect. Throughout their sometimes difficult history, the Vietnamese people have proven to be clever, resilient, hardworking, family-centric, gracious, and joyful.

The food of Vietnam reflects the history, climate, and geography of the country as well as the spirit of the populace. The country is situated in Southeast Asia, roughly between 9 degrees and 22 degrees north of the equator, giving it a tropical to subtropical climate. That, along with some variation in altitude and two monsoon seasons affording it an abundance of water in most locations, has created a diverse selection and bounty of ingredients, many available year-round. In the north, anchored by the dignified ancient capital city of Hanoi, there is the agricultural bounty of the Red River Delta region, the far-northern hills and mountains with several all-but-isolated hill tribe groups, and the coastline that runs north to south the entire length of the country. The North has the greatest influence from China and more of a preference for wheat over rice as a food staple than in the south. The food in the north tends to be a bit more austere than its southern counterpart, utilizing a simpler array of seasonings and a more conservative approach, but flavor and sophistication are not lacking by any means.

The central portion of Vietnam contains an agrarian base, and Hue was the royal seat in the past. This royal gastronomy tradition continues to be sustained, and its somewhat closely guarded secrets mark one of the finer cuisines of the world. The royal cuisine stills exerts some influences in the central region even today; from home cooking to street and market stalls and restaurants, the portions tend to be smaller with a larger array of plates offered, reminiscent of the bounty laid out for the emperor and his court. The cooks in the central area also favor some bold flavors such as chiles, fermented shrimp sauce, and pickled items. Peanuts are often used as a garnish.

In the south, cosmopolitan Ho Chi Minh City (formerly Saigon) is the largest metropolitan area, and it is teeming with over six million residents. The south enjoys a warm and tropical climate year-round and includes the fertile Mekong Delta and the coastline, dotted with fishing villages and a new influx of seaside and island resorts. The cooking there is rice-based and includes fresh fruits and a large assortment of vegetables as well as a vast array of seafood delicacies. Outside influences have been freely incorporated into the exuberant cooking of the south. Dishes from other parts of Southeast Asia, India, China, and the West all make appearances on the tables of the south or at least lend some flavors and techniques to inform the cooking here.

In general, Vietnamese cooking is a tantalizing blend of clean, fresh, bright, sweet, and hot flavors. Steaming, stewing, and grilling techniques are more common than frying. Fresh herbs and hot chiles play an important role. The aspects of flavor, aroma, texture, color, contrast, balance, and even the sound a food makes are all taken into consideration in the planning and creation of a Vietnamese meal. This simple, agricultural-based peasant cuisine has been infused with a gracious and unpretentious sophistication through the European influence of the French and the royal cuisine of Hue, as evidenced in part by the first-rate baguette available nearly everywhere around the nation. Today's Vietnamese cooking has been informed and shaped into its unique identity through its history, climate, and geography and, perhaps more than anything else, by the tenacious, resourceful, creative, clever, and gracious people of that country.

INGREDIENTS

Many cooks are daunted by the unfamiliar ingredients called for in foreign cuisine. Vietnamese cooking has a whole array of these, but the truth is, a good number of authentic dishes may be produced with only a few essentials. The following describes these basic ingredients along with many others that are occasionally called for. It is becoming increasingly easier to obtain many of these things through local markets and by mail order. You should not give up on a recipe when you cannot find a certain ingredient unless the recipe specifies that you absolutely cannot prepare the dish without it. Vietnamese cooking is flexible, and I have witnessed many Vietnamese cooks freely substituting when they cook. This type of cooking is about freshness, layers of complementary and contrasting flavors, and a pleasing outcome. Use your intuition when confronted with an ingredient dilemma, and you will be fine.

SAUCES

Essential to Vietnamese cooking, prepared sauces are used in the cooking process and also as a table condiment.

FISH SAUCE [Nuoc Mam]

Fish sauce is absolutely essential to the Vietnamese kitchen and the table. While often strange and unfamiliar to the Western palate, an appreciation is usually gained after a bit of exposure. Nuoc Mam adds a salty fermented richness that not only seasons the food but also ties the flavors together in a way that gives the dish completeness. It is used in cooking and finishing dishes and as a table condiment, either straight or mixed with other ingredients, as in Nuoc Cham. Fish sauce falls into the category of flavors known in Japanese as umami, along with mushrooms, soy and Worcestershire sauce, miso, and other fermented items that add a subtle, esoteric, and satisfying component to food.

The brands produced in Vietnam, particularly from the island of Phu Quoc and from Phan Thiet and Nha Trang, are many. The quality of the domestic fish sauces is superior to most produced in other countries, although there are several from Thailand that are produced in the "Vietnamese style" and possess the lighter, more complex, and sophisticated flavors that are so prized.

Soy sauce may be substituted when a vegetarian dish is required or if Nuoc Mam is just too strong for your tastes, but I encourage you to try it. You may start with a mix of soy and Nuoc Mam to start you on the path of enjoying this incredible condiment.

SOY SAUCE [Nuoc Tuong]

Used for stir-fries, vegetarian dishes, marinades, and dipping, soy sauce is not as common as fish sauce, but is used fairly often. Try to use a Vietnamese or Chinese light soy sauce.

BEAN SAUCE [Tuong Hot]

A sharp-edged sauce made from fermented soybeans is used for sauces and stir-fries and is often cooked for a dipping sauce.

HOISIN SAUCE [Sot Tuong]

Sweeter than bean sauce with aromatic spices, hoisin is Chinese in origin but is often used in Vietnamese cooking for dipping sauces, stir-fries, and marinades; in the southern part of the country, it is frequently added to Pho at the table.

CHILE PASTE [Tuong Ot Toi]

Made from ground red chiles and sometimes with garlic added, this sauce is important for cooking and is also used as a table condiment.

OYSTER SAUCE [Dau Hao]

Often used to flavor vegetable dishes and other Chinese-style preparations, oyster sauce adds a richness and saltiness to foods. It also clings well to the ingredients, giving them a nice shiny luster.

SHRIMP SAUCE [Mam Ruoc or Mam Tom]

A pungent, purplish paste that is used to add richness and saltiness to sauces, stews, soups, and dipping sauces, shrimp sauce is very popular in the central region around Hue.

ANCHOVY SAUCE [Mam Nem]

An extremely aromatic and pungent condiment, anchovy sauce is used to add a powerful fermented fish flavor to some dishes, and it is diluted with water and/or vinegar for a dipping sauce.

COCONUT MILK [Nuoc Cot Dua]

Used in desserts, curries, vegetable dishes, and some dipping sauces, coconut milk can be made fresh, as it usually is in Vietnam, or you can buy it canned in most supermarkets. Make sure to buy the unsweetened variety.

SPICES

These pantry staples will add color and flavor to many dishes; they keep well, so they are easy to have around.

ANNATTO SEEDS [Hat Dieu]

A New World ingredient, annatto seed is a natural reddish-orange food colorant with a subtle flavor that the Vietnamese have assimilated into several dishes, like Bo Kho. Either it is ground or the seeds are fried in oil to extract their color and flavor.

TURMERIC [Bot Nghe]

A rhizome root in the ginger family, turmeric is used both fresh and as a dry powder for curries and marinades, as in Cha Ca. It imparts an intense yellow color and a slightly astringent flavor to food.

GINGER [Gung]

Often used with seafood and some meats and in Chinese-style dishes, ginger is also important for medicinal purposes.

SUGAR [Mia]

Used in all its forms, cane sugar is very important in cooking. It is often caramelized to add bittersweet richness to sauces and marinades. Yellow rock sugar, a combination of white and brown sugar with honey, can be found at many Asian and Chinese markets. Caramelized sugar is a suitable replacement.

FIVE-SPICE POWDER [Bot Ngu Vi Huong or Huong Lieu]

Chinese in origin, it is popular for seasoning grilled meats and clay-pot stews. The five spices often vary but usually include star anise, cinnamon, cloves, some kind of pepper (often Sichuan), and anise or fennel seeds.

GALANGAL [Gieng]

Another root in the ginger family, galangal has a floral character. When dried, it is used in soups, stews, and marinades; in the south, it is often used fresh in Thai-influenced curries.

STAR ANISE [Boi Huong, Dai Hoi, or Tai Hoi]

Star anise, the dried pod of a tree grown mainly in northern Vietnam, originated in China. The aromatic flavor has a licorice taste similar to anise, only stronger, and is used in soups, especially Pho.

CINNAMON [Bot Que or Que Chi]

Used sometimes to scent soups and stews and to flavor desserts, Vietnamese cinnamon has a strong distinctive flavor and is an essential ingredient in five-spice powder.

WHOLE CLOVES [Dinh Huong]

Used in soups and marinades, cloves are also one of the ingredients in five-spice powder.

CURRY POWDER [Bot Ca-ri]

Vietnamese curry powder is a bright yellow from lots of turmeric and is fairly spicy. I use a Madras style if I cannot find the Vietnamese version.

DRIED RED CHILE FLAKES [Ot Kho]

Used in marinades and some stir-fries, these chiles are hot.

FRESH HERBS

Fresh herbs are a quintessential part of the Vietnamese diet. They are added to cooked dishes as well as salads and are usually offered at the table, allowing each diner to complete his or her plate as they like with additional layers of flavors.

CILANTRO OR CORIANDER [Ngo]

Cilantro, or coriander, is the most widely used culinary herb in the world. It adds a bright flavor and green color to many Vietnamese dishes and is found on most tables in Vietnam.

DILL [Rau Thi La]

Dill, unlike most herbs in Vietnamese cookery, is usually cooked. It appears in several pâté-like meat recipes and in Cha Ca Hanoi.

MINT [Rau Hung Lui or Hung Kay]

Mint adds a sweet and aromatic component to many fresh rolls, soups, and grilled dishes. Hung Lui is similar to spearmint and Hung Kay is a spicier version that often has a reddish tinge to the stems.

RED PERILLA [Rau Tia To]

Related to the Japanese shiso, red perilla has a flavor that is reminiscent of mint, citrus, and a touch of cinnamon. The leaves are generally two-toned, green on one side and purple-red on the other. It is usually served along with strongly flavored foods and is almost a requisite for Banh Xeo (sizzling crêpes) and with Bun Cha.

ASIAN BASIL OR THAI BASIL [Hung Que or Rau Que]

This basil has a strong cinnamon, clove, and anise scent, and is served with Pho, other soups like Bun Bo Hue, noodle dishes, and many grilled items. It is also known as cinnamon basil or Mexican basil. You could substitute Mediterranean varieties, but they are much stronger and sweeter, so be careful.

VIETNAMESE CORIANDER [Rau Ram]

Unique to Southeast Asia, Rau Rahm (also known as hot mint) is peppery and very herbal, and has notes of cilantro. It is used as a garnish or on the ubiquitous herb/ lettuce plate on the table.

CULANTRO [Mui Tau]

A sawtooth-edged, spear-shaped leaf identifies this herb, which is native to Latin America and the Caribbean. It has an earthy cilantro-like flavor but is much stronger. Used in sour soups and some stews, it is a real treat to have as a garnish for Pho.

CHIVES [Hoa Hue]

The chives most commonly used in Vietnamese cooking are Chinese chives, fairly thin with a flower bud at the end. They taste slightly of garlic. Substitute other chives or scallions.

RICE PADDY HERB [Ngo Om or Rau Om]

Often hard to come by, this exotic herb can be grown in your garden. It has a perfumed cumin-like scent. Used in sour fish soup and sweet and sour dishes, it could be substituted with ground cumin seeds and fresh cilantro.

LEMONGRASS [Xa]

Lemongrass is found in many Vietnamese dishes and is used in marinades, soups, stews, stir-fries, and curries. The wider bulbous end toward the root is used. An outer layer is peeled off, then it is crushed, finely chopped, or sectioned for longer-cooking dishes.

VIETNAMESE BALM OR GREEN PERILLA [Rau Kinh Gioi]

Actually a relative of lemon balm rather than red perilla, Vietnamese balm has a pronounced lemongrass-like flavor and aroma with light green, oval-shaped, serrated-edged leaves. Shredded into noodle dishes, soups, and salads, it is usually served with Bun Cha.

FISH MINT [Rau Diep Ca]

A most unusual culinary herb, fish mint has a strong acidic or sour flavor up front that quickly transforms into a fishy taste. Despite these strong flavors, it lacks much aroma. Even the Vietnamese are divided on their love or hate of this one. It is served with the table garnishes for grilled meats and fish dishes.

BETEL OR PEPPER LEAF [La Lot]

This heart-shaped leaf from a plant in the pepper family requires heat to release its peppery aromatic flavors. It is shredded into soups and stir-fries and is wrapped around meats for grilling.

NOODLES

There is a wide assortment of noodles available in Vietnamese cookery. These are a few of the most common.

RICE VERMICELLI [Bun]

Thin dry noodles that only need a short cooking time, they are used in soups and salads, and are served with grilled meat dishes like Bun Cha.

RICE STICKS [Ban Pho]

These noodles come in various widths ranging from narrow to wide. They are featured in soups and stir-fries, and are usually soaked before they are cooked.

EGG NOODLES OR CHINESE NOODLES [Mi]

These are thin wheat-flour noodles that are used in Chinese-style stir-fries and some soups.

BEAN THREAD, CELLOPHANE, OR GLASS NOODLES [Mien]

Used in soups, salads, and stir-fries, these are also used to fill several types of rolls.

RICE PAPER [Banh Trang]

Yes, rice paper is a noodle, as it is made in the same way and with the same ingredients as a rice noodle, just not cut so narrowly. After steaming on a silk cloth over a pot of boiling water, the noodles are carefully transferred to a bamboo mat to dry in the sun, which causes their characteristic cross-hatched pattern. Some brands add tapioca starch to achieve elasticity and to make them more transparent. Look for thin transparent ones, available in many shapes and sizes.

OTHER INGREDIENTS

PEANUTS [Lac or Dau Phong]
Usually roasted and chopped, peanuts appear in many dishes, often as a garnish.

RICE [Gao]
Gao Thom, or long-grained jasmine rice, is the variety most often used in Vietnamese cooking. There are many brands available. It is called Gao when raw and Com when it has been cooked.

STICKY OR GLUTINOUS RICE [Gao Nep]
Also known as sweet rice, it is used in Banh, steamed cakes, breakfast porridges, and desserts. When cooked and ready to eat, this rice is called Xoi.

RICE FLOUR [Bot Gao]
Rice flour is used for noodles, crêpes, cakes, and sometimes for thickening.

BANANA LEAVES [La Chuoi]
Used to wrap foods for steaming or grilling and sometimes used as a serving medium, banana leaves impart a subtle flavor to food. Often available frozen in Asian and Latin American markets.

TAMARIND PASTE [Me]
Tamarind paste is the sticky material from the tamarind pod that holds the seed in place. The seeds are removed, and the paste needs to be mixed with a little hot water to soften. Strain before using. Tamarind adds a tart flavor and a caramel-like color to soups and stir-fries as well as some barbecue dishes.

EQUIPMENT, UTENSILS, AND TABLE SETTINGS

Most of the equipment and utensils that you need for cooking Vietnamese food is probably already in your kitchen, but there are a few items that are important or will make life easier for you if you have the right ones.

FOR THE KITCHEN

POTS AND PANS

Use an array of sauté pans or skillets; heavy is better, and one or two with a lid will be helpful. Saucepans, including a larger one like a Dutch oven, also come in handy. If you are going to make some of the soups or make your own stock or broth, a stockpot or kettle that holds 8 to 12 quarts is important.

WOK

While not absolutely necessary (a skillet can do most of the same things), a wok is a handy tool that is useful for stir-frying, steaming, and deep-frying. I like a heavy steel model with a lid (no nonstick please—it is not necessary).

STEAMER

Very important in Vietnamese kitchens, although it may be improvised, a good steamer makes it a lot easier. The Asian steamers seem to be the best, but some other models also work well. I prefer metal to bamboo for ease of cleaning, but they work about the same. Do not get a steamer with holes too large or too small; about half an inch or a touch less in diameter is about right. A tight-fitting lid is also important.

KNIVES

Good sharp knives are important, as Vietnamese cooking involves a lot of cutting, slicing, and chopping. A cleaver and a chef knife are handy to have around. A paring knife is also essential. Those three will serve you well, but you could also consider a boning knife, a slicer, a Shoku knife (or sushi knife), etc.—that is up to you.

FOOD PROCESSING

A mortar and pestle can be very useful for crushing spices and making pastes. A food processor can do some of the same as well as chopping and some slicing and shredding. A mini chopper can also handle the chopping of things like garlic, ginger, and shallots, but a knife works fine too.

MANDOLIN

I like a mandolin—a slicing, cutting, and shredding tool—that is very sharp and precise. It is quite a time-saver. The classic French ones are more expensive, but many of the Asian versions cost a lot less and work just as well, if not better.

RICE COOKER

A great luxury item but not a necessity, an electric rice cooker is a simple and virtually fool-proof method of cooking rice and does not tie up your stove. I have been cooking rice for years in a saucepan, and I am satisfied with that method. The choice is yours.

FOR THE TABLE

CHOPSTICKS

A very important part of Vietnamese eating, chopsticks allow you to pick up bite-sized pieces of food from the typical communal serving dishes on the table. There are many choices out there. I prefer the type that are not too thin and slick. A little friction and some size make it easier to hold onto the food.

SMALL BOWLS OR DISHES

These are used for individual servings of dipping sauces.

RICE BOWLS

Individual rice bowls are usually placed at each setting on the Vietnamese table. It gives a place for the food to "land" when serving oneself from the communal dishes. The rice gets flavored by placing food on it before you eat it. The rice bowls should not be too large, sized to fit comfortably in the palm of the hand. Rice bowls may also be used to hold dipping sauces for communal use.

SOUP BOWLS

Rice bowl sizes work fine for soups in a multicourse meal, but for main dish soups like Pho or Bun Bo Hue, you will need something larger (a 24-ounce capacity or larger) that can hold the entire serving. A deeper style is preferred, as it makes it easier to get at the noodles with chopsticks without making a mess.

SPOONS

Teaspoons are used for stirring beverages like coffee and tea, and for serving dipping sauces and condiments. Larger soupspoons, either Asian-style or traditional, are necessary for eating soup. Large serving spoons are useful for rice and for dishing up some main courses, and ladles are needed for soups.

PLATES AND PLATTERS

Small to medium plates are often set at each place to be used for wrapping things and/or as a place to discard items like bones, shells, squeezed limes, etc. Larger plates and platters can be used to serve the main courses. A slightly concave shape or an upwardly curved rim helps to hold the sauces on the platter.

SERVING BOWLS

Serving bowls of several sizes can be useful for holding foods like rice, noodles, main courses, side dishes, and soups.

The Vietnamese table would be considered pretty bare without at least one dipping sauce present. Many dishes in the culinary repertoire of Vietnam are subtly flavored, and the individual diners then use the dipping sauces and condiments to enhance the seasonings to their taste. These table dipping sauces also add a fresh and sometimes contrasting note to the cooked dish. Every cook has favorites, and the variations are many. Here are some of the basic ones along with some of my favorites.

DIPPING SAUCES & CONDIMENTS

THE RECIPES

Soy-Lime Dipping Sauce
[Nuoc Tuong Pha Gung]

1 (2-inch) piece peeled ginger
¼ cup warm water

2 tablespoons sugar
⅓ cup soy sauce

3 tablespoons fresh lime juice
Sliced Thai or serrano
  chiles, as desired

∞ MAKES 1 CUP ∞

USED FOR VEGETARIAN meals, this sauce may also be used instead of a fish sauce–based dip or alongside as an alternative. I like it with vegetables too.

I Slice the ginger thinly and then cut across the slices to make thin matchsticks. Combine the water and sugar, stirring until sugar is dissolved. Mix everything together and serve. This sauce is typically made fresh for each meal, but leftovers will keep several days in the refrigerator.

Salt, Pepper, and Lime Dipping Sauce
[Muoi Tieu Chanh]

Coarse kosher or sea salt Freshly ground white or black pepper	Lime wedges	Thinly sliced or minced serrano or Thai chiles (optional)

∽ MAKES 1 CUP ∾

A SIMPLE TABLE condiment that replaces the ubiquitous salt-and-pepper shakers of Western tables, Muoi Tieu Chanh is used for simple boiled, steamed, or grilled meats, seafood, poultry, and vegetables. It can be presented in individual dishes for each diner or in a communal bowl. The components are placed separately in the dish and then mixed together with the end of a chopstick to make a savory paste for dipping. Both white and black pepper is used according to taste preferences, and chiles are an option as well. The proportion of salt to pepper and the amount of lime juice is also a matter of preference. If you can find key limes or Mexican limes, the pale-yellow variety with seeds, try them for a slightly sweeter taste. Often, fresh chile slices are added along with or instead of the pepper in this condiment.

I Mix together the salt and pepper, and then moisten with some lime juice. Add the chiles, if desired, mix with a chopstick, and serve.

SWEET CHILE SAUCE

[NUOC SOT CHUA NGOT]

2 tablespoons cornstarch
  or arrowroot powder
1¾ cups water, divided
4 tablespoons white or raw sugar
2 tablespoons finely minced
  shallot or onion

2 cloves garlic, smashed and peeled
2½ tablespoons rice or white vinegar
2 tablespoons fish sauce or soy
  sauce (or a combination of both)
Generous dash of salt
¼ teaspoon finely ground white pepper

½ teaspoon ground annatto
  seeds (optional)
2 tablespoons finely grated carrot
1 tablespoon finely grated scallion
1–2 tablespoons minced red
  serrano or Thai chile, or 2
  tablespoons sweet red pepper

∽ MAKES 2 CUPS ∽

A SORT OF Vietnamese sweet-and-sour sauce, this recipe is more sophisticated and lighter than the Chinese and Thai versions. Sweet chile sauce is usually served with crispy spring rolls and other roll-up dishes, grilled meats, seafood, and anything else you like. It can be made with or without the chiles. I like to caramelize the sugar first to give the flavor more depth, but it is still tasty without that step. If you want the reddish-orange color of the commercial types, add the annatto seeds; otherwise, the sauce will have a light, somewhat transparent color.

1 Mix the cornstarch with 3 tablespoons cool water to dissolve and set aside.

2 In a heavy saucepan, caramelize the sugar until a light golden-brown (see page 40 for technique). Add the remaining water, shallot, garlic, vinegar, fish sauce, salt, pepper, annatto seeds, carrot, scallion, and chiles to the pan. Bring to a boil, and stir for 1–2 minutes to dissolve the sugar (it will crystallize at first). Serve immediately or store in the refrigerator.

THE PEOPLE AND FLAVORS OF HUE AND HOI AN

The food in Hue is unique and very special. The legacy of the emperors is still evident in a wide variety of small plates and portions served with a fastidious attention to detail. The locals enjoy strong flavors with chiles, fermented shrimp paste, and sauces playing an important role. There is seasonality to the cuisine, and many temperate climate vegetables and fruits are produced here during the cooler seasons. Nowhere can you better observe this bounty of produce than at Dong Ba market alongside the north bank of the Perfume River next to the storied and colorfully lighted Trang Thien Bridge. Everything is available in this massive marketplace: clothes, hats, cloth, incense, jewelry, household utensils and necessities, kitschy curios and trinkets, fruits, vegetables, meats, live poultry and seafood, condiments, flowers, and just about anything else you can think of. Under the roof of the main building are the permanent vendors, usually carrying dry goods and equipment, but some sell fruits as well. Around the fringes are a myriad of people from the countryside, hawking their colorful basketfuls of herbs, vegetables, chiles, fruits, vegetables, etc., with the fresh fish vendors on the outer edge paralleling the river. This is also a friendly market, and a smile and some sign language will go a long way in exploring and negotiating.

The Hoi An fish market is a sight to behold. Starting at well before dawn, the fishing boats motor in to unload their overnight catch, and

often there are so many that they merely tie up to each other in a giant raft formation rather than waiting for a space alongside the dock. The eager buyers swarm over these boats, haggling over price and quality, and when a deal is struck, they hurry to the shore to set up and sell again to the waiting smaller buyers. This market is dominated by women, and it is quite a sight to see the conical hats bobbing and the high-pitched voices negotiating and arguing in musical Vietnamese. Many different varieties of fish, shellfish, and other exotic marine creatures are on display, depending on the time of year.

A number of villages that surround Hoi An

in the countryside specialize in different crops to be sold in the local market and in Da Nang. One special place is the cooperative village of Tra Que, where they produce organic herbs and vegetables, all fertilized with seaweed. The flavors of these herbs and greens are noticeably stronger and tastier than the already-flavorful typical ones seen around the rest of the country. The market in Hoi An is a great place to view, taste, and buy the local harvest, and there you can also purchase a Hoi An specialty: fresh Cau Lau noodles, made with rice flour, water, and a touch of ashes, which causes the trademark yellow color.

CARAMEL SAUCE
[NUOC HANG]

½ cup water
¾ cup white or raw sugar

 MAKES 2 CUPS

USED TO ADD a sweet and slightly bitter richness and color to stews and clay-pot dishes, and for marinades on grilled meats, this is a very important sauce in the Vietnamese cooking repertoire. Its subtle flavoring is often added to other sauces, and it adds nuances of flavor that are distinctive to the Vietnamese style of cooking. You can also find this sauce premade in the bottle at Asian markets.

1 Preheat a heavy saucepan or skillet to medium-high heat.

2 In a separate pan or in a cup in the microwave, heat the water to almost boiling. Place the sugar in the preheated pan and it will begin to melt. Stir by tilting the pan in various directions as needed (using a spoon could cause the sugar to re-crystallize). Be careful not to burn the sugar.

3 When the sugar is melted and has reached a dark golden-brown color with a little smoke rising from the surface, remove from the heat and carefully add the very hot water to the pan. The water will sizzle and hiss—take care not to burn yourself. Return the pan to the heat and cook until all the sugar is dissolved. Cool and use as called for. The sauce may be stored at room temperature for a few weeks in a tightly sealed jar.

Coconut Peanut Sauce with Chiles

[Tuong Den]

1½ cups fresh coconut milk, or 1 can (12 ounces) unsweetened coconut milk

Dash of salt

2 tablespoons hoisin sauce or spicy bean paste

⅓ cup Basic Vietnamese Dipping Sauce (page 42) or Soy-Lime Dipping Sauce (page 32)

3 tablespoons roasted and chopped peanuts

1–2 tablespoons Chile-Garlic-Oil Table Condiment (page 44) or mashed fresh red serrano or Thai chiles

---

⌘ MAKES ABOUT 1¾ CUPS ⌘

THIS IS A sauce that I tasted in the Mekong Delta, where coconuts grow everywhere. It was served with a rice paper roll filled with a salad of shredded vegetables and herbs and grilled meats similar to the Grilled Beef and Shrimp Hand Rolls (page 58). It is also good with fried squid and shrimp and any grilled meat, poultry, or seafood. Often made with fermented soybeans, I use Nuoc Cham and a little hoisin sauce with good results.

I Mix the coconut milk, salt, hoisin sauce, and dipping sauce together well. Bring to a boil in a saucepan and then simmer for about 5 minutes to thicken slightly; let cool. Pour into a large serving bowl, sprinkle with peanuts, and then spoon the chile condiment or fresh chiles in the center. (You may also pour sauce into individual dipping bowls and distribute the peanuts and chiles among them.) The chiles are stirred into the sauce as desired by each individual. Serve at room temperature but store in the refrigerator.

BASIC VIETNAMESE DIPPING SAUCE
[NUOC CHAM]

³⁄₄ cup warm water	¼ cup lime juice or rice vinegar	1 clove garlic, peeled and
3–4 tablespoons sugar	2–3 Thai chiles, or 1–2 serrano	sliced (optional)
½ cup fish sauce	chiles (red or green), thinly sliced	

∞ MAKES 2 CUPS ∞

A REQUIREMENT AT every Vietnamese table, Nuoc Cham is used to season grilled and steamed meats, salad and fried rolls, vegetables and seafood. It is used in many recipes, too, but is always put on the table for each individual to dip as their taste dictates. This recipe has a distinct southern Vietnam influence with the addition of lime juice, water, and sugar. You may also use rice vinegar instead of all or part of the lime juice for a variation. In the central and northern regions, Nuoc Cham is often made using only the fish sauce and chiles, perhaps with just a touch of sugar.

For those of you who are challenged by the flavor of fish sauce, try substituting two-thirds of the fish sauce with soy sauce. The next time, try a little less soy and more fish sauce, and you will be ready for the real thing before long.

I Mix the water and sugar, stirring until the sugar is dissolved. Combine with the rest of the ingredients and serve. This sauce is typically made fresh for each meal, but leftovers will keep several days in the refrigerator.

CHILE-GARLIC-OIL TABLE CONDIMENT
[OT TOI]

1–2 teaspoons hot red chile flakes	¼ teaspoon salt
12–15 cloves garlic, peeled	½ cup vegetable oil, divided

∞ MAKES ALMOST 1 CUP ∞

A REGULAR ON many Vietnamese tables, this condiment is for those who want a touch of subtle chile and garlic flavor to add to noodles, soups, and other dipping sauces. It also can be added to marinades for extra zip. It is usually made with dried chiles, but I also offer an option made with fresh ones that is a bit sharper like the many jarred sauces that are available.

1 Smash the chile flakes, garlic, salt, and 4 tablespoons oil in a mortar and pestle, or chop finely in a food processor. Combine with the rest of the oil and heat in a small saucepan over low heat until it bubbles. Continue cooking for 5 minutes, stirring occasionally; cool and serve. Store at room temperature. This condiment will keep for several weeks.

Variation: To make this recipe with fresh chiles, replace the chile flakes with 1 tablespoon chopped red serrano or Thai chiles and carefully add 1 tablespoon rice or white vinegar to the mixture after it is cooked. Stir well to combine.

SCALLION OIL
[MO HANH]

¾ cup vegetable oil
Pinch of salt

6 medium scallions (mostly
   the green part, but some
   white is fine), thinly sliced

☙ MAKES ABOUT 1¾ CUPS ❧

USED TO GARNISH many dishes and to flavor soups, noodles, vegetables, salads, rice, grilled and boiled meats, etc., this oil is a nice addition to the arsenal of flavors on the Vietnamese table.

1 Heat the oil in a saucepan until fairly hot, about 350 degrees. Add the salt and scallions, and stir for 15 seconds while cooking. Carefully transfer into a room-temperature heatproof bowl to accelerate the cooling process and stir every few minutes to help with the cooling. Serve at room temperature and store sealed in the refrigerator. (Oil may be refrigerated but should be served at room temperature for best flavor.)

PICKLED GARLIC AND CHILES
[OT NGAM GIAM]

| 1/3 cup sugar
1 tablespoon kosher or sea salt | 1 cup rice or white vinegar
8–12 serrano, Thai, or jalapeño chiles,
red, green, or a mixture of the two | 12–14 cloves garlic, peeled |

∽ MAKES ABOUT 1½ CUPS ∽

THESE CHILES AND garlic are served with noodle soups as well as with many rice dishes. In fact, they are great with just about anything. The blanching helps to take the sharp edge off the garlic and chile flavors, and also keeps the color bright.

I Mix the sugar, salt, and vinegar in a nonreactive bowl and stir until sugar is dissolved. Slice the chiles into 1/8- to 1/4-inch pieces; set aside. Place the garlic in boiling water for 15 seconds, then add the chiles and boil 10–15 seconds more. Drain, immediately place in the vinegar mixture, and stir. Allow to cool, place in a glass jar or other nonreactive container with a tight-fitting lid, and refrigerate for 24–48 hours before using. May be kept for several weeks in the refrigerator.

MARINADE FOR GRILLED MEATS
[Nuoc Sot]

¼ cup hoisin sauce

3 tablespoons fish sauce or soy sauce

2 tablespoons lime juice or vinegar

½ teaspoon ground black pepper

1 teaspoon sugar

¼ teaspoon salt

1 teaspoon Chile-Garlic-Oil Table Condiment (page 44); 1 teaspoon chile-garlic paste; or 1 clove garlic, crushed and mixed with ½ teaspoon dry red chile flakes

1 teaspoon vegetable oil or toasted sesame oil

2 teaspoons finely minced lemongrass or ginger (optional)

¼ teaspoon five-spice powder (optional)

⌁ MAKES ENOUGH TO MARINATE 1–2 POUNDS MEAT ⌁

THIS BASIC CHINESE-INFLUENCED marinade works well for seasoning meats that are to be grilled, particularly beef or pork. It adds a sweet and tangy flavor, and creates a light glaze on the meat when cooked. If applied to the meat at least 1 hour before cooking, it will also help tenderize it.

I Mix all of the ingredients together before applying to the meat. The marinade will keep in the refrigerator for several days.

These dishes are eaten as snacks rather than first courses on Vietnamese tables, but could be used as appetizers or side dishes in a menu with courses. They represent only a few of the many snack-like dishes that are usually seen at curbside eateries and Vietnamese beer pubs. They can be eaten as a light lunch with one of the beverages as well.

APPETIZERS, SNACKS & BEVERAGES

THE RECIPES

Grilled Lemongrass Beef Skewers
[Thit Bo Nuong Xa]

MARINADE
4 tablespoons minced lemongrass
2 tablespoons minced shallot
1–2 teaspoons minced hot chiles
   or chile paste (optional)
1 tablespoon fish sauce

1 teaspoon shrimp sauce
   or hoisin sauce
Dash of salt
¼ teaspoon ground black pepper
2 teaspoons raw or brown sugar
1 teaspoon toasted sesame oil (optional)
1 tablespoon vegetable oil

BEEF SKEWERS
1½ pounds sirloin, top round, or
   chuck steak, sliced ¼ inch thick and
   cut into strips about 3 x 1 inches
24–32 bamboo or wooden skewers

⌒ MAKES 24–32 SKEWERS, ENOUGH FOR 8–10 APPETIZERS OR 4–6 MAIN COURSES ⌒

THIS APPETIZER OR snack is a well-known specialty of the central regions around Hue, Da Nang, and Hoi An, but you will find versions throughout the country. I once had a delicious version made with pork at a street stall operated by three lovely young ladies in Sapa, the far north of Vietnam. Shrimp sauce may be used here for extra richness, but if you do not have it or find it too strong for your taste, just use the hoisin option or omit it altogether.

In Vietnam, these skewers are cooked over charcoal, and a direct flame method is definitely preferred to provide that smoky flavor. These tasty skewers may be part of a full meal or, when served with a salad and some rice, they can make a great lunch or dinner.

1 Mix the marinade ingredients together and then combine with the meat, taking care to coat all surfaces. Cover and marinate for at least 1 hour and up to 24 hours. (If marinating for more than 1 hour, refrigerate and remove from the refrigerator at least 30 minutes before cooking.)

2 Soak the wooden skewers in hot water for at least 30 minutes to prevent burning. Preheat a charcoal or gas grill to medium high. Thread 1–2 pieces of the beef on each skewer and place on the grill. Cook for 3–4 minutes per side until browned and a bit blackened around the edges. Serve immediately with Basic Vietnamese Dipping Sauce (page 42); Salt, Pepper, and Lime Dipping Sauce (page 33); or other favorite dipping sauce.

SOUTHERN-STYLE SALAD HAND ROLLS
[GOI CUON]

16–18 rice paper rounds (8–9
    inches in diameter)
16–18 leaves lettuce (butter or leaf)
½ pound cooked and sliced pork
    (leftover grilled pork is great
    here) or cooked ground pork
¼–⅓ pound rice vermicelli, cooked
    in boiling water for 4–5 minutes just

until done, then rinsed in cool water
2–3 scallions (green part only),
    cut into 1-inch sections
1–2 medium carrots,
    peeled and grated
16–18 cilantro sprigs
16–18 fresh mint sprigs or other

Vietnamese herbs like Asian basil
½–¾ pound cooked small or medium
    shrimp, cut in half lengthwise
1 cup bean sprouts (optional)
Basic Vietnamese Dipping
    Sauce (page 42) or Soy-Lime
    Dipping Sauce (page 32)
Sweet Chile Sauce (page 34) (optional)

☙ MAKES 16–18 ROLLS ☙

CONSIDERED BY MANY non-Vietnamese to be one of the standard items of Vietnamese cooking, these rolls are often labeled as spring or summer rolls, more properly a name for a Chinese roll using wheat-flour wrappers. These rolls, however, reflect the fresh tastes of Vietnamese food, and the ingredients used are flexible, allowing for what is on hand or for leftovers.

1 Dip a rice paper in a bowl of warm water for a few seconds, blot it dry on a towel, and place it on a plate or other work surface. Place a lettuce leaf in the lower center of the rice paper. Top with some of the pork, noodles, scallions, carrots, cilantro, and other herbs. Fold the bottom flap of the paper over the filling, and then roll one turn away from you. Place some of the shrimp and bean sprouts, if using, on the rice paper in front of the roll and turn again. (This is so that the shrimp and bean sprouts can be seen from the outside of the roll). Fold each side flap to meet in the center, slightly overlapping. Roll the wrap away from you to form a sealed roll. Serve immediately with your choice of dipping sauces.

Many cooks are daunted by the unfamiliar ingredients called for in foreign cuisine. Vietnamese cooking has a whole array of these, but the truth is, a good number of authentic dishes may be produced with only a few essentials.

STUFFED SQUID
[MUC NHOI THIT]

2 ounces cellophane noodles (bean thread)	½ pound minced or ground pork	½ teaspoon sugar
¾ ounce dried tree ear or other Chinese mushrooms (the amount should loosely fill a ¾-cup measure)	1 teaspoon minced lemongrass or ginger	¼–½ teaspoon dry chile flakes (optional)
	1 tablespoon fish sauce	⅓ cup vegetable oil
12 squid, approximately 4–6 inches long	2 teaspoons lime juice	Soy-Lime Dipping Sauce (page 32) or Basic Vietnamese
	½ cup finely chopped scallions	Dipping Sauce (page 42)
	¼ teaspoon ground pepper	

☙ SERVES 6–10 AS AN APPETIZER OR 4–6 AS A MAIN COURSE ☙

OF COURSE, FRESH squid is preferred for this recipe, but I have had good results with frozen squid too. You may also substitute minced chicken or shrimp for the pork here for an interesting variation.

1 Soak the noodles in hot water until soft and just edible, drain and rinse in cold water, and then cut into bite-size lengths. (Do not let noodles get too soft as they will be cooked more in a later step.)

2 Soak the mushrooms in boiling water until pliable, about 10–15 minutes, and then remove the stems and chop finely.

3 Clean the squid, and if there are any tentacles, chop them finely and add them to the filling.

4 Mix together the pork, mushrooms, lemongrass, fish sauce, lime juice, scallions, pepper, sugar, and chile flakes, and then mix in the noodles. Poke a small hole in the narrow end of each squid as an air vent to allow stuffing. Fill each squid body, loosely, leaving about ½ inch at one end. Close the end and secure with a toothpick. Heat the oil in a pan (you may want a deep pan here to prevent splattering oil), then sear the squid for 2–3 minutes, or until some color develops. Reduce the heat slightly and braise for 8–10 minutes more, or until the filling is fairly firm and the outside is a deep golden brown. Drain and allow to rest for several minutes to firm the filling. Remove the toothpicks and slice in bite-size pieces, about ¼ inch thick. Serve with dipping sauces.

Madam Huy's Stuffed Clams

[Con Trai Huy]

2½ pounds fresh medium-size clams	1 shallot, peeled and minced	4 ounces peeled small shrimp
½ cup cold water	1 teaspoon sugar	1 tablespoon fish sauce
1 (2-inch) piece ginger, peeled and sliced into quarters, each slice gently flattened with the side of a knife to release the flavor	1 ounce pork fatback or bacon, chopped	1 egg, separated
	½ ounce dry tree ear mushrooms, rehydrated in very hot water, stems removed, and chopped	1–2 tablespoons vegetable oil
1½ teaspoons salt, divided		¼ teaspoon black pepper
		2 limes, juiced

SERVES 2–3

MADAM HUY IS an amazing woman who I met in Hue city. She is a chef whose expertise lies in Imperial Cuisine, and on our first meeting, we spent hours just talking food, bouncing around from halting English to French to rapid-fire Vietnamese translated by a friend. Although there was a definite language barrier, we seemed to understand each other when it came to cooking and our feelings about good food. Huy sent this recipe to me; it is one that she featured at a special Vietnamese menu she prepared at the Hanoi Opera Hilton last year.

1 Rinse the clams, then open them and remove the meat. Scrape out the shells, wash, and reserve.
2 Place the water, ginger, and 1 teaspoon salt in a bowl. Add the clams, mix well, and soak for 15 minutes. Drain and rinse with cold water. Remove the ginger and pat the clams dry with a towel.

2 In a mortar, pound the shallot, sugar, and clams to make a paste. Add the pork fat, mushrooms, and shrimp, and continue pounding until smooth. Mix in the fish sauce and egg white well. (You may also do this by pulsing in a food processor.)

3 Oil the inside of the cleaned clamshells and place 1½ teaspoons of the clam mixture in each one. Steam in a steamer for 5 minutes, remove the cover, and brush the top of each filling with some beaten egg yolk. Return to the steamer, cover and cook 2–3 minutes more, or until the mixture has set and is cooked through. Mix together the remaining salt, pepper, and lime juice, and pour some over each stuffed clam. Serve immediately.

GRILLED BEEF AND SHRIMP HAND ROLLS

[BO NUONG TOM CUON]

1 pound beef chuck, sirloin, or
   top round, sliced into 1/4-inch-
   thick sheets (or less*)
Marinade for Grilled Meats (page 47)

18–20 rice paper rounds (8–9 inches
   in diameter)
18–20 lettuce leaves (butter,
   red, or green leaf lettuce)

1/2 pound small-to-medium
   cooked shrimp
1/2 pound jicama
1–2 scallions, cut into 1 1/2-inch
   sections, then finely cut
   lengthwise into thin slices
2 medium carrots, peeled
   and thinly julienned
1 medium sweet red bell pepper,
   thinly julienned (optional)

Enough 2-inch-long cilantro sprigs
   to place 1 or 2 in each roll
Basil, mint, red perilla, or
   other Vietnamese herbs, as
   available or as desired
Basic Vietnamese Dipping
   Sauce (page 42) or Soy-Lime
   Dipping Sauce (page 32)
Sweet Chile Sauce (page 34) (optional)

∽ MAKES 18–20 ROLLS ∽

THESE HAND ROLLS are one of my takes on the many salad rolls made with uncooked rice paper that you will find served as snacks, appetizers, and light meals by street vendors, in restaurants, and in homes, particularly in the southern part of Vietnam. This recipe draws its inspiration from a Saigon street version that stir-fries ground beef, jicama, dried shrimp, eggs, and sometimes sausages. This one uses grilled sliced beef, which adds an interesting texture and a subtle smoky flavor. I leave the jicama raw rather than sautéing it so that it remains very crunchy. Many different combinations of fillings may be used for fresh hand rolls. The rolls may be made before serving, or the components may be placed on the table for guests to make their own.

1 Marinate the beef slices in the marinade for at least 30 minutes. Grill beef and slice into 1/4-inch strips.

2 Dip a rice paper in a bowl of warm water for a few seconds, blot it dry on a towel, and place it on a plate or other work surface. Place a lettuce leaf in the lower center of the rice paper. Top with some of the sliced beef, shrimp, jicama, scallions, carrots, bell pepper, cilantro, and other herbs. Fold the bottom flap of the paper over the filling, then fold each side flap to meet in the center, slightly overlapping. Roll the wrap away from you to form a sealed roll. Serve immediately with your choice of dipping sauces.

* You may also place thicker slices between two sheets of plastic wrap and carefully pound it to the desired thickness with a kitchen mallet.

CRISPY ROLLS WITH SALAD WRAP
[CHA GIO OR NEM RAN]

1 egg
2 tablespoons fish sauce
4 tablespoons sugar, divided
¼ teaspoon salt
1 clove garlic, minced
½ teaspoon ground white
  or black pepper
1½ ounces cellophane noodles
  (bean thread, usually 1 bundle),
  soaked in hot water for about 20
  minutes until soft and pliable,
  drained, and cut into 1-inch pieces

5–6 dried wood-ear or shiitake
  mushrooms, reconstituted in
  very hot water and minced
¼ cup minced scallions
½ cup finely minced white onion
½ cup grated taro root or jicama
  (squeeze out the excess
  water if using jicama)
¼ cup finely shredded carrots
½ pound ground pork
4 ounces cooked shrimp, chopped
4 ounces cooked crabmeat

2 quarts warm water
24 or more rice paper rounds
  (8–10 inches in diameter)
Vegetable oil
24 lettuce leaves
Mixed herbs
1½ cups bean sprouts
1 cup grated carrots (optional)
1 medium cucumber, thinly sliced
Basic Vietnamese Dipping
  Sauce (page 42)
Sweet Chile Sauce (page 34)

❧ MAKES ABOUT 2 DOZEN ROLLS ❧

IT WAS TEMPTING to give in and employ the not-so-correct but commonly used term "spring rolls" for this dish; however, I resisted since they are known in Vietnam as Nem Ran in the north and Cha Gio in the south, and spring roll is actually a Chinese dish using wheat-flour wrappers. Whatever moniker you use for them, these scrumptious appetizers are certainly all the rage, both in Vietnam as well as in the U.S. and Europe. For many westerners, it is the defining recipe of Vietnamese cuisine, although in Vietnam it is not considered quite that important. This recipe calls for pork, shrimp, and crab, but you could easily prepare these using only one or two of the three meats.

1 Beat the egg, fish sauce, 1 tablespoon sugar, salt, garlic, and pepper together until smooth. Stir in the noodles, mushrooms, scallions, onion, taro root, carrots, pork, shrimp, and crabmeat; mix well.

continued on page 62

2 Mix the warm water with the remaining sugar in a wide bowl. Lay a smooth towel on the counter, dip a rice paper in the water for a few seconds, drain well, and then lay on the towel. Repeat with another rice paper so that you can roll 2 in succession.

3 Place 2 generous tablespoons of the filling in the center of the bottom third of the rice paper and roughly shape into a cylinder. Fold the bottom edge of the paper to cover the filling. Carefully fold one side edge to overlap the first fold. Repeat with the other side. Gently roll away from you to make a cylinder, making sure not to trap any air inside the roll. Place seam side down on an oiled tray and repeat until all of the filling is used.

4 Put enough oil into a deep skillet or large saucepan to a depth of 2 inches. Heat to 350–365 degrees. Fry the rolls a few at a time, turning occasionally, until golden brown on all sides, about 4–6 minutes. Drain on paper towels, cut if they are large, and serve immediately with lettuce, herbs, and remaining vegetables to wrap them in and dipping sauces.

TEA

[TRA]

| 2 cups water plus ¼–⅓ cup to warm the pot | 2–3 tablespoons (½- to ¾-ounce) loose green or black tea, | jasmine, or other varieties |

◌ MAKES 1 POT, ENOUGH FOR 4–6 CUPS ◌

TEA OR TRA (pronounced cha) is probably the most important beverage in Vietnam. In outlying rural regions with questionable water supplies, boiling water to make tea helps to ensure that it is free of bacteria and parasites. Green tea is the most commonly consumed, while black tea is also regularly enjoyed. In the southern regions of the country, the tea is usually a green jasmine variety that is naturally slightly sweet; in the north, the preference runs towards a slightly bitter, more astringent selection. Some prefer it straight and others take sugar. Tea is consumed before, during, and after meals, and can be readily purchased from street vendors. Many Vietnamese coffeehouses routinely serve complementary tea along with a cup of coffee, as it is considered a palate cleanser.

1 Bring the water to a boil. Rinse a heavy teapot with the extra boiled water to warm it up and then discard that water. Place the loose tea in the tea pot and add 2 cups water. NOTE: The water should not be boiling when you add it to the tea, as this causes bitterness.

2 Place the lid on the teapot and allow to steep for 4–5 minutes. Pour into glasses, sweeten with sugar or honey if desired, and enjoy.

VIETNAMESE COFFEE
[CA PHE]

| 1–2 tablespoons sweetened condensed milk (optional) | 3 level tablespoons freshly ground dark-roast coffee | beans (about 1 1/2 ounces) 3/4 cup water |

∽ MAKES 1 CUP ∽

THE FRENCH PLANTED coffee beans in Vietnam, and the plantations were a big contributor to the income of these colonial occupiers. The legacy continues as Vietnam recently moved into the No. 2 position among world coffee-exporting countries. The people of Vietnam inherited the taste for rich, darkly roasted coffee beans from the French, and coffee vendors can be found on almost every street; it closely rivals tea in popularity. Coffee is usually brewed with individual drip-through gadgets that sit on top of the cup. Any sweetener or flavoring is first placed in the cup, then the brewer is loaded with finely ground, dark-roast coffee and set on top of the cup or glass. Boiling water is poured in the brewer, and a lid is placed on top. It sometimes seems to take a long time for the water to drip slowly through the coffee grounds, but the result is a rich, almost syrupy thick, delightful brew that is incredibly satisfying. The classic choices are Ca Phe (straight coffee), Ca Phe Sua (coffee with sweetened condensed milk), Ca Phe Da (coffee with ice) and Ca Phe Sua Da (iced coffee with sweetened condensed milk). Vietnamese beans taste great, but any high-quality French or other dark roast is fine.

1 Put the sweetened condensed milk, if using, in the bottom of a glass that will hold 8 ounces or more of liquid.

2 Place the coffee in the brewing device. Screw down the screen that holds the grounds in place, snug but not too tight. Set on top of the glass or cup. Pour boiling water slowly into the brewer over the top of the grounds. Place the lid on top and let the water drip through the coffee. When all of the coffee has dripped into the glass or cup, remove the brewer, stir, and enjoy.

Salads are an excellent expression of the Vietnamese cooking style: crunchy, fresh, the juxtaposition of sweet, sour, and hot flavors along with beautiful colors and presentation. Many other dishes in the Vietnamese culinary repertoire also seem to contain components of salads. Many of these recipes can serve a dual purpose, as a part of a multicourse meal or as a stand-alone meal. Please enjoy the following recipes and also use them as your inspiration to create salads of your own.

SALADS

THE RECIPES

CUCUMBER AND SHRIMP SALAD
[GOI OR NOM DUA CHUOI]

$1/3$–$1/2$ pound thinly sliced beefsteak, sirloin, chuck, or top round

$1/2$ recipe Marinade for Grilled Meats (page 47); or a combination of 2 tablespoons fish sauce or soy sauce, 1 teaspoon chile garlic paste, 1 teaspoon chopped ginger, 1 teaspoon sugar, and 1 tablespoon vinegar

2 pounds cucumbers (English or hothouse varieties work best, as they do not need peeling), sliced in half lengthwise and seeded

1 medium-to-large carrot, peeled and julienned with a knife

1 small-to-medium white or red onion, peeled and cut in half, thinly sliced to produce half-moon slivers

2 teaspoons salt

1 teaspoon sugar

DRESSING

$1/4$ cup fresh lime juice

1 tablespoon rice or distilled white vinegar

$1/4$ cup fish sauce

1 tablespoon water

3 tablespoons sugar

$1/2$ teaspoon ground black pepper

1 teaspoon finely minced shallots

1–2 serrano or Thai chiles, thinly sliced

1 cup cooked and shredded chicken breast

$3/4$ cup cooked small shrimp

$1/3$–$1/2$ cup chopped roasted peanuts

Lettuce or cabbage leaves for the base of the salad (optional)

☞ SERVES 4–6 AS A MAIN DISH OR MORE AS PART OF A LARGER MEAL ☜

I FIRST TASTED this dish at the Folk Song Restaurant on Hue. I was having dinner with Ms. Huy, an Imperial cuisine chef and culinary school instructor, and several university students, who have since graduated and become good friends. Typical of a popular Vietnamese salad, this recipe is often served when there are special guests or for celebrations. While this one calls for a combination of shrimp, chicken, and beef, it can certainly be prepared using only one or two of those components. I have also seen this salad made using pork instead of beef. However, some protein is important to provide richness that contrasts with the crunchy bright flavors of the vegetables.

1 Place the beef in the marinade; set aside.

2 Thinly slice the cucumbers and place them in a bowl with the carrot and onion slices. Toss with salt and sugar; let sit for about 20 minutes, then drain and thoroughly rinse in cold running water. Gently squeeze the excess moisture out of the vegetables a few at a time using a smooth cloth towel.

3 Mix all of the dressing ingredients together; set aside.

4 Cook the marinated beef on a grill or sear in a large pan with just a touch of oil. When cooled, slice into thin strips by cutting across the grain of the meat. Place the meat, chicken, shrimp, and vegetables in a bowl with half of the peanuts and toss together. Add the dressing and toss again.

5 Place the salad on a serving plate lined with lettuce or cabbage leaves, if using, and top with the remaining peanuts.

POMELO AND CHAR-GRILLED SHRIMP SALAD
[GOI BUOI]

1 tablespoon fish sauce
1 teaspoon soy sauce
2 teaspoons minced shallot or scallion
½ teaspoon ground white
  or black pepper
1 teaspoon sugar
18–24 medium shrimp, peeled
  and deveined, tails left on

2 tablespoons vegetable oil
½ cup julienned carrots
½ cup julienned cucumber that
  has been peeled and seeded
1 pomelo, peeled and segmented,
  then cut into bite-size pieces
30 Vietnamese or Thai basil
  leaves, shredded

2 tablespoons coarsely
  chopped cilantro
1 red serrano, jalapeño, or Thai
  bird's-eye chile, minced
1 cup Basic Vietnamese
  Dipping Sauce (page 42)
¼ cup chopped roasted peanuts

∽ SERVES 6 ∽

THIS REFRESHING SALAD juxtaposes the sweet-tart flavor of the pomelo, a larger and sweeter cousin of the grapefruit, with the savory smokiness of grilled shrimp, all enhanced by the fragrance of the cilantro and basil along with the crunchy peanuts. Serve it as part of a multicourse meal or as a lunch or light supper main course. If you cannot find pomelo, substitute the sweetest grapefruit that you can find.

1 Soak six to ten bamboo or wooden skewers in hot water for about 30 minutes; set aside.

2 Mix the fish sauce, soy sauce, shallot, pepper, and sugar with the shrimp; let marinate for 20–30 minutes, then add the oil and toss.

3 Soak the carrots and cucumber in lightly salted ice water for 20 minutes and drain.

4 Place the shrimp on the skewers and grill over high heat just until done. Toss the carrots, cucumber, pomelo, basil, cilantro, chile, and dipping sauce in a bowl, then add the cooked shrimp and toss gently. Arrange on a platter or in individual servings and sprinkle the peanuts over the top. Serve immediately.

One could explore and taste the food in Hanoi for years and not yet experience all there is to offer.

CUCUMBER AND TOMATO BASIC SALAD
[NOM CHUA NGOT]

1 large or 2 medium English cucumbers, or 6 pickling cucumbers	3 tablespoons rice or distilled white vinegar	1½ tablespoons minced shallots
2–3 well-ripened medium tomatoes, sliced and then cut in half to make half-moon shapes	2 tablespoons lime juice	½–1 red or green serrano or Thai chile, thinly sliced (optional)
	2–4 cloves garlic, crushed and minced	2 teaspoons vegetable oil (optional)
	2 tablespoons sugar	⅛ cup cilantro leaves
	½ teaspoon salt	Freshly ground black pepper (optional)

☙ SERVES 4–6 ☙

THIS IS A case where simple ingredients come together to create a stunning dish that makes a wonderful accompaniment to many other recipes, particularly rich stews and grilled meats or seafood. I often order a version of this when I am dining in Vietnam, and I almost always make it for my table at home. The key is good cucumbers and tomatoes—don't even attempt to use the pinkish winter tomatoes and the standard waxed cucumbers from most supermarkets, or you will be disappointed. The dressing is designed to bring out the flavors in fresh foods and not to hide them. I also find myself dipping a tomato or cucumber slice from this salad into the dipping sauce on the table for an extra burst of salty flavor. The vegetable oil is a Western option but does add a nice flavor balance and gives the salad some shine. I sometimes add freshly ground black pepper just before serving.

1 Peel the cucumbers, or not, as you wish, then thinly slice and arrange on a plate with the tomatoes.

2 Mix the vinegar, lime juice, garlic, sugar, salt, shallots, and chile in a bowl, and let sit for a few minutes to allow the flavors to mingle. Whisk in the oil, if using, and pour over the tomatoes and cucumbers. To garnish, sprinkle on the cilantro and black pepper, if using, and serve.

SHRIMP, PORK, AND CABBAGE SALAD

[GOI TOM THIT]

¼ head (about ⅓ pound) green cabbage	Dash of salt	½ English or hothouse cucumber, or 2–3 pickling cucumbers, thinly sliced
1 medium carrot, peeled	1 tablespoon water	24 leaves Vietnamese coriander or Asian basil, cut in half (or omit and triple the amount of cilantro called for)
½ medium red or white onion, peeled and very thinly sliced	1 or 2 serrano or Thai chiles, sliced (optional)	
¼ cup lime juice	4 ounces cooked small or large shrimp, coarsely chopped	
2 tablespoons fish sauce	4–6 ounces cooked pork, thinly sliced into bite-size pieces	1 tablespoon coarsely chopped cilantro
2 tablespoons sugar		¼ cup chopped roasted peanuts

⏤ SERVES 4 AS A LIGHT MEAL OR 6–8 AS PART OF A LARGER MEAL ⏤

EASY TO MAKE and a great outlet for leftover meat, this salad and its many variations is popular throughout the country. Feel free to use cooked chicken, beef, fish, and other seafood in place of the shrimp and pork. You can also vary the herbs and add other greens as well as using chiles, or not, as it suits you. Very thinly sliced vegetables are the hallmark of this salad and they give a refreshing crunch to go along with the meats.

1 Slice the cabbage very thinly, then cut the carrot into a very thin julienne about 2 inches long; place both in a bowl with very cold water to cover and place in the refrigerator to soak and crisp for 20–30 minutes.

2 Combine the onion, lime juice, fish sauce, sugar, salt, water, and chiles in a bowl; place the shrimp and pork in this dressing to marinate 10 to 15 minutes before assembling the salad.

3 Drain the carrots and cabbage, then pat dry with a towel or dry in a salad spinner. Add to the dressing along with the cucumber, herbs, and half of the peanuts; toss well. Place on a serving dish and top with the remaining peanuts.

SPICY CABBAGE AND CHICKEN SALAD

[GOI CAI BAP GA]

½ clove garlic, peeled

1 small shallot bulb, peeled

¼ teaspoon salt

1–2 serrano or Thai chiles, stems removed and coarsely chopped

1 teaspoon sugar

¼ cup rice vinegar or distilled white vinegar

2 tablespoons fish sauce

1 tablespoon soy sauce

Juice of 1 lime

⅛ cup chopped cilantro, Vietnamese coriander, or Asian basil

2 tablespoons vegetable oil (optional)

8–10 ounces cooked and shredded chicken

1 medium-to-large carrot, peeled and shredded or finely julienned

1 medium red onion, peeled and thinly sliced*

12 ounces cabbage (1 small head or about ½ medium head), cored and cut into strips no wider than ½ inch

1 or 2 scallions, cut into 2-inch sections and finely julienned

☞ SERVES 4 AS A MAIN DISH OR 6–8 AS PART OF A LARGER MEAL ☜

THIS TASTY SALAD is a great lunch or light supper main course on a hot summer day. In Vietnam, a salad such as this may be served with soup, and diners often will combine the two. The sweet, sour, and spicy hot balance of flavors in the dressing complement the slight bitterness of the cabbage, and the entire salad is a textural delight. Shrimp or crab could be used instead of the chicken, and the vegetarian version is also nice. I like Savoy cabbage for this dish, as it is a bit milder, and I prefer the texture; however, any variety of cabbage will work well, including purple cabbage for a color contrast.

1 Crush the garlic, shallot, salt, and chiles in a mortar and pestle until they form a paste. (If you do not have a mortar and pestle, chop everything together as fine as possible, smash with the blade of your knife, and then chop again.)

2 Mix the chile-garlic paste with the sugar, vinegar, fish sauce, soy sauce, lime juice, and herbs. Let sit for a few minutes to mingle the flavors, then whisk in the oil, if using.

3 Toss the dressing in a bowl with the chicken, carrot, onion, and cabbage, and transfer to a serving plate or dish. Garnish with the scallions.

* After slicing, rinse briefly in hot water and then again in cold water to remove the "hot" taste.

THE PEOPLE AND FLAVORS OF HANOI

One could explore and taste the food in Hanoi for years and not yet experience all there is to offer. International and Vietnamese restaurants abound, and the street-side choices are endless. The French influence still holds more sway here than in other parts of the country, but a more global awareness of food seems to be creeping in. The most well-known dishes from Hanoi are Pho, Bun Cha, Cha Ca, and Banh Cuon, but there are countless other specialties waiting to be discovered. Pho, a beef soup with rice noodles, is often consumed for breakfast and has become the national dish of Vietnam. Granted, in the south you are served more condiments and a wider variety of herbs to go with Pho, but in Hanoi it is all about the broth. Here, it is rich and aromatic, taking more than twenty-four hours to prepare, and its flavor is subtly complex—certainly a legacy from the French cooks. Bun Cha, grilled pork slices and patties served in a warm, slightly sweet and sour fish sauce broth with rice vermicelli and an accompanying plate of herbs and lettuce, is the quintessential street food of Hanoi. Banh Cuon is a square or round sheet of fresh rice noodle wrapped around various fillings, from ground pork and/or mushrooms topped with fried shallots to char-grilled beef, herbs, and lettuces called Pho or Bo Cuon, like the vendors on the north side of Truc Bac Lake have offered for the past several years. Cha Ca, a special fish dish that was originally conceived at the Cha Ca la Vong

restaurant many years ago, has become so popular
and is offered by many clones of this still-operating

where this dish is widely available are named
Cha Ca street. Another great place to sample

Vietnamese fare is the Com shop. *Com* means rice but can also refer to a meal. These are the diners of Vietnam, where you can point at any number of offerings and create a plate accompanied by rice that will satisfy and fill you for a few dollars at the most.

GREEN MANGO SALAD WITH GRILLED BEEF

[GOI XOAI VOI BO NUONG]

⅛ cup finely minced lemongrass, about 2 medium stalks

1 tablespoon minced shallot

1 tablespoon fish sauce

1 teaspoon soy sauce

1½ teaspoons sugar

½ teaspoon chile paste with garlic (optional)

10–12 ounces sirloin, strip, or chuck steak, sliced about ¼ inch thick

2 green mangoes or unripe mangoes (about 1½ pounds), peeled and sliced about ⅛ inch thick, then cut into ½-inch-wide strips

1 red bell pepper, stemmed, seeded, inner membranes removed, and cut into ¼-inch-wide julienne

¼ cup Basic Vietnamese Dipping Sauce (page 42) mixed with the juice of 1 lime and 1 or 2 well-crushed or finely minced serrano or Thai chiles

About 24 Asian basil leaves

⅛ cup chopped cilantro

2–3 shallots, peeled and thinly sliced, with the rings separated and then sautéed in some vegetable oil until golden brown and crispy

1 scallion, cut into 2-inch sections and julienned

❧ SERVES 4–6 ❧

I HAVE ENJOYED versions of this salad at several different contemporary restaurants around Vietnam. The green mangoes used there are a special variety that is meant to be eaten green; however, I have had good luck with using regular mangoes that are a bit under ripe, and the added sweetness is a nice addition to the salad. You could also substitute tart apples or even jicama.

1 Mix the lemongrass, shallot, fish sauce, soy sauce, sugar, and chile paste, and marinate the beef in this mixture for 30–40 minutes. Grill the beef over medium-high heat, let rest a few minutes, and then slice across the grain into ¼-inch-wide strips. **NOTE:** You may also use ½ recipe Marinade for Grilled Meats (page 47) in place of the above marinade ingredients.

2 Toss the mango and bell pepper with the dipping sauce mixture, then add the basil, cilantro, and beef. Place on a serving dish and garnish with the fried shallots and scallion.

BANANA FLOWER SALAD WITH DRIED BEEF AND SQUID
[NOM HOA CHUOI BO MUC KHO]

1 banana flower (about 1 pound)
Vinegar
2 ounces dried squid
3 ounces dried beef (jerky)
1 clove garlic, peeled
1 (2-inch) section
   lemongrass, chopped

1 tablespoon rice or distilled
   white vinegar
1/4 cup lime juice
2 teaspoons sugar
1/2 teaspoon ground black
   or white pepper
2 tablespoons fish sauce
1/4 cup coarsely chopped Vietnamese
   balm, cilantro, or Asian basil

1/4 head red or green cabbage,
   sliced into thin strips
1 small-to-medium red onion,
   peeled and sliced into thin strips*
1/2 red bell pepper, thinly julienned
1 cup sliced fresh pineapple (1/2-inch-
   wide and 1/8-inch-thick strips)

◌ SERVES 4 AS A MAIN DISH OR 6–8 AS PART OF A LARGER MEAL ◌

DRIED SQUID IS often hawked by street vendors with a pushcart on the streets of many Vietnamese cities. The squid is usually toasted slightly on a flame, then either put through a roller or pounded to tenderize it before it is eaten as a snack. My friend Khai, the chef of his family's Dzoan Restaurant in Saigon, first introduced me to the idea of a salad using both dried beef and dried squid. I added the banana flowers, as I feel the sharp astringency contrasts nicely with the richness of the dried meats. Use a firm banana blossom that is tightly closed. If you cannot find banana flowers, increase the cabbage accordingly and still enjoy this salad. The addition of pineapple lends an extra sweetness, but you can also omit it.

I Cut off the banana flower stem, slice it in half lengthwise, and then remove whitish core. Cut into 2-inch lengths, then julienne about 1/4-inch wide. Immerse the pieces in boiling salted water for about

continued on page 88

10–15 seconds and then immediately rinse in cold water until cool. Sprinkle with a little vinegar and set aside.

2 Toast the squid directly over a stove burner on high until a slight color change develops. Pound the squid slightly with a kitchen mallet to tenderize, taking care not to break it up; slice into thin slices.

3 Thinly slice the dried beef similar in size to the squid slices.

4 Crush the garlic and lemongrass together in a mortar and pestle until a paste is formed. Mix the paste with the vinegar, lime juice, sugar, pepper, fish sauce, and herbs. Toss the dressing with the cabbage, onion, beef, squid, bell pepper, pineapple, and banana flower stem and transfer to a serving plate.

* After slicing, rinse briefly in hot water and then again in cold water to remove the "hot" taste.

The Vietnamese consume an amazing quantity of noodles. Many noodles are found in soups, stir-fries, salads, and even crispy fried rolls. The majority of noodles consumed are made from rice or a mixture of rice and tapioca; however, wheat noodles are also used frequently. In Vietnam, fresh noodles are widely available, whether homemade or purchased at the markets or from street vendors. In the West, you can often find fresh noodles at Asian markets, but many times, you will need to resort to dried noodle varieties.

SOUPS &
NOODLE
DISHES

THE RECIPES

CHICKEN AND GLASS NOODLE SOUP
[MIEN GA]

1½ tablespoons yellow rock sugar, or 1 tablespoon white refined sugar and 2 teaspoons honey 1 clove garlic, minced 2 tablespoons shallots, minced 3 tablespoons fish sauce or soy sauce (or a combination of the two) 4 quarts chicken broth	½ cup tree ear or other dried or fresh mushrooms, sliced in thin strips (about 5–6 dried mushrooms, reconstituted by covering with boiling water, soaking for 15–20 minutes, draining, and removing the stems) 1 or 2 sliced or julienned red serrano, jalapeño, Fresno, or Thai chiles (optional)	1½ to 1¾ pounds cooked chicken meat (the amount that a 2¼-pound fryer will yield), hand shredded or cut into bite-size chunks Giblets from 1 chicken, cooked and finely chopped (optional) 2 scallions, cut into ½-inch sections 12 ounces glass noodles (cellophane), soaked in very hot water until just softened, drained, and rinsed in cool water ⅓ cup chopped cilantro or Vietnamese coriander leaves (optional)

∞ SERVES 6 AS A MAIN DISH OR MORE AS PART OF A LARGER MEAL ∞

THIS RECIPE IS relatively simple to make; you can either use already-made or store-bought chicken broth (beware of the saltiness) and leftover precooked chicken, or you can make your own stock (see recipe on page 105) using a small chicken, reserving the meat for the soup.

1 In a heavy preheated pot or Dutch oven, add the sugar and caramelize slightly until a light golden brown; add the garlic and shallots, stir for a moment, and then add the fish sauce and broth.

2 Bring the broth to a boil, then add the mushrooms and chiles. Boil for 1 minute and then add the chicken and giblets, if using. When the broth returns to a boil, add the scallions and noodles, and bring to a boil again; remove from the heat, taste for seasoning, add salt or fish sauce as needed, stir in the herbs, and serve.

BEEF NOODLE SOUP
[PHO BO]

BROTH AND MEAT

6 pounds beef soup bones
2 pounds trimmed beef—brisket,
   boneless leg, chuck, round,
   or sirloin—cut in half
2 white onions
6 cloves garlic
1 (1½-inch) piece ginger, peeled
   and cut into 3 to 4 slices
8 quarts water
¼ cup fish sauce
1 tablespoon salt
4 good-sized stalks lemongrass,
   lightly bruised and cut
   into 2-inch pieces
8–10 whole black peppercorns,
   lightly toasted

4 tablespoons yellow rock
   sugar, or 3 tablespoons
   Caramel Sauce (page 40)
2 carrots, peeled and cut into thirds
3 stalks celery, cut into thirds
10 star anise, lightly toasted
8 whole cloves, lightly toasted
1 (3-inch) cinnamon stick (optional)

TO FINISH

2 pounds flat rice noodles or other
   rice noodles, cooked in boiling
   water just until done, strained,
   and then rinsed in cool water
10 to 12 ounces very thinly sliced beef
   sirloin, chuck, tenderloin, or brisket
2 to 3 cups fresh bean sprouts

GARNISHES

Lime wedges
1 white onion, peeled and
   very thinly sliced
3 scallions, thinly sliced on the bias
Fresh cilantro, Asian basil,
   mint, culantro, perilla,
   Vietnamese coriander, etc.
Thinly sliced serrano or Thai chiles
Lettuce leaves
Chile sauce
Hoisin sauce
Pickled garlic and chiles

☞ SERVES 8 ☜

PHO IS PROBABLY the most recognized and widely discussed Vietnamese dish. Pronounced "fer," with the "r" barely audible with a slight dip and then rise in the tone, this dish probably owes its roots to the French culinary sensibility and obsession with good-quality stocks as well as the Chinese contribution of noodles and seasonings; however, in the hands of Vietnamese cooks, it is transformed into something with an identity all its own and has practically become the national dish. While Pho Bo (beef pho) is the most common, Pho Ga (chicken pho) is also available. To make that version, you will need a rich chicken stock scented with the same aromatics and cooked chicken meat.

I Place the beef bones and brisket in a large pot and cover with cold water. Bring the water to a boil and cook

continued on page 98

for 5 minutes. Remove from the heat and immediately drain; then rinse the meat and bones in cool water; drain again. Cut a piece of the brisket into 4 or 5 chunks.

2 Char the onions, garlic, and ginger over a direct flame until fairly blackened and fragrant, about 3 minutes for the garlic, 4–5 minutes for the ginger, and 6–8 minutes for the onion. Cool to the touch, remove the skins, and discard. Cut the onion and ginger into several pieces.

3 Place the 8 quarts water in a large pot and add the bones, beef, onion, garlic, ginger, fish sauce, salt, lemongrass, peppercorns, rock sugar, carrots, and celery. Bring to a boil, then reduce to a simmer and cook for 1½ hours, occasionally skimming any scum that rises to the surface. Remove the large piece of brisket from the broth and immerse in cold water for 10 min-

utes to cool and preserve the color; drain and set aside to be thinly sliced and added to the soup when serving. Continue simmering the broth for another 45 minutes. Add the star anise, cloves, and cinnamon, and simmer another 45 minutes. Turn off the heat and allow to cool for 30 minutes. Skim the excess fat that rises to the top and discard. Strain the soup through a fine mesh strainer or cheesecloth and reheat to serve. Taste for seasoning and add more salt if needed. It should taste fairly salty, as the noodles and garnishes have no salt.

4 Reheat the noodles and bean sprouts separately in a pot of boiling water and place a portion in each bowl. Place some of the raw and cooked meat slices on top of the noodles. Ladle about 1½ to 2 cups of nearly boiling broth in each bowl and serve immediately, along with the garnishes.

RICE VERMICELLI WITH SALAD AND HERBS
[BUN VOI RAU THOM]

12 ounces rice vermicelli
8–10 leaves lettuce (butter, red or green leaf, or romaine), torn into bite-size pieces

½ cup mixed herb leaves (red or green perilla, cilantro, Vietnamese coriander, mint, fish balm, etc.), cut larger leaves into halves or thirds
¼ cup Asian basil leaves

1 cup peeled, seeded, and julienned cucumber
1 cup bean sprouts
½ cup grated carrots (optional)

∽ SERVES ABOUT 4 ∾

THESE NOODLES COMBINED with herbs and crunchy salad ingredients are often the base for grilled or stir-fried meats, tofu, or seafood, and sometimes meat and hot broth are added to them to make a soup; however, with a bit of Basic Vietnamese Dipping Sauce (page 42) or other dipping sauce, they could make a light meal or salad all on their own. The noodles are served cold or, rather, at room temperature, so they may be cooked ahead of time and rinsed well to cool and prevent stickiness.

1 Cook the noodles in boiling water until just done but still a bit firm. Rinse in cool water until the water runs clear and the noodles are cooled; drain well.

2 Mix the lettuce, herbs, and vegetables together and place in bowls topped with some of the noodles, or place in communal bowls for guests to assemble themselves. Serve with toppings or several dipping sauces (pages 29–47).

Vietnam is a country that has a long and colorful history. It was first populated by a variety of indigenous groups, many who are still evident today. Throughout their sometimes difficult history, the Vietnamese people have proven to be clever, resilient, hardworking, family-centric, gracious, and joyful.

HANOI-STYLE GRILLED PORK WITH RICE NOODLES

[BUN CHA HANOI]

TRADITIONAL MARINADE

1 large shallot, peeled
  and finely minced
2 scallions, thinly sliced
  crosswise to make rings
1 tablespoon sugar
1 tablespoon Caramel Sauce (page 40),
  or 2 teaspoons raw or brown sugar
2 tablespoons fish sauce
¼ teaspoon salt
½ teaspoon ground black pepper
½ teaspoon five spice
  powder (optional)

MEAT AND NOODLES

1½ pounds pork shoulder, trimmed
  and sliced about ¼ inch thick or less
  and then cut into bite-size pieces (if
  you want to omit the ground pork
  patties, increase this to 2½ pounds)
2 tablespoons vegetable oil
12 ounces ground pork (optional)
½ white onion, finely chopped
  (optional if omitting the ground pork)
12 ounces rice vermicelli, cooked
  al dente about 4–5 minutes, then
  rinsed in cool water and drained

GARNISHES

Lettuce leaves
Fresh herbs (mint, red perilla,
  cilantro, Asian basil, culantro,
  and Vietnamese balm)
Cucumber slices and/or bean sprouts
Sliced fresh chiles
Chopped fresh garlic
2 recipes of Basic Vietnamese
  Dipping Sauce (page 42), with
  1 cup additional water added

∞ SERVES 6 AS A MAIN DISH OR MORE AS PART OF A LARGER MEAL ∞

THIS SIMPLE STREET food is by far my favorite Vietnamese meal. It contains all of the savory goodness, fresh flavors, and contrasting textures that are embodied in the cuisine. Along with the savory grilled pork slices or pork belly and spicy patties of ground meat is a simple plate of cold rice noodles, a platter or basket containing fresh lettuce leaves, an array of pungent herbs, and a bowl of Basic Vietnamese Dipping Sauce where it is all mixed together. No elaborate meal that I have enjoyed at any upscale eatery has ever satisfied me so well or beckoned me back as powerfully as Bun Cha in Hanoi. Some of these vendors serve only the sliced pork, but most accompany it with a ground pork patty. I will give you both recipes and you can decide how far to go. Crispy Rolls with Salad Wrap (page 60), are usually offered to accompany Bun Cha. Cut into bite-size pieces, they are dipped in the broth and eaten with chopsticks.

I Mix together all of the marinade ingredients, except the oil and divide equally between two bowls.

continued on page 104

NOTE: You may also use the recipe for Marinade for Grilled Meats (page 47) for a nontraditional but equally tasty result.

2 Place the sliced pork in one bowl with the marinade, mix well, add the oil and mix again; marinate for 20–30 minutes.

3 Place the ground pork and onion in the other bowl, mix well, and shape into 2-inch-round patties that are about ¼ inch thick. Start a gas or charcoal grill. Cook the pork slices and the patties until cooked through and slightly crispy around the edges.

4 Set the table with a plate of vermicelli and a plate with all the garnishes in the center. Provide a bowl with warmed dipping sauce to mix the noodles with the vegetables, herbs, pork pieces, chiles, garlic, and patties.

CHICKEN FOR SOUP OR BROTH
[NUOC DUNG GA]

1 (2-to-3-pound) chicken	2 ribs celery	3–4 inches lemongrass, lightly smashed
5 quarts water, approximately	1 white onion	1–2 star anise
2 carrots, peeled	2 cloves garlic, peeled	1 teaspoon whole peppercorns
	1–2 inches ginger, peeled and sliced	

∽ MAKES ABOUT 1 GALLON ∽

THIS IS A basic method for cooking a whole chicken to produce broth and meat to be used in soups and other dishes. It can be prepared using only the chicken and the water, but adding the optional ingredients makes for a more interesting and deeply flavored result.

1 Rinse the chicken and place in a pot large enough to hold the bird, water, and other ingredients.

2 Add enough water to cover the bird with an extra inch or two and heat slowly to boiling. Remove from heat and skim off and discard any foam that collects on the surface of the water. Add the vegetables and seasonings, and bring to a boil again; turn down to a simmer for 15 minutes and then turn off the heat; let sit 20 minutes more.

3 Remove chicken from pot and let cool enough to handle. Remove the skin and discard; strip the meat off the bones and reserve for another use. Put the bones back into the pot and bring to a boil. Reduce heat until just boiling and cook another 45 minutes, adding water as needed to maintain about 4 quarts liquid. Remove from heat and cool, skim off any excess fat, and then strain stock into a container. Store in the refrigerator or freezer until ready to use.

HUE-STYLE NOODLE SOUP WITH BEEF, PORK, AND MEATBALLS
[BUN BO HUE]

4 pounds beef soup bones, or
  2 pounds beef bones and
  2 pounds pork neck bones
1 pound boneless pork leg,
  skin and fat still attached
2 pounds boneless beef shank or
  trimmed brisket, cut in half
1/3 cup vegetable oil, divided
1 white onion, peeled and
  coarsely chopped
1 tablespoon annatto seeds
Salt and black pepper
6 quarts water
4 stalks lemongrass, divided
4 tablespoons fish sauce, divided
1 large shallot, peeled and minced
4 cloves garlic, minced

2–3 tablespoons dry red chile flakes
1 tablespoon shrimp sauce (optional)
2 tablespoons raw or brown sugar

MEATBALLS
1 pound ground pork
1 tablespoon minced shallot
1 clove garlic, minced
1 scallion, minced
2 teaspoons fish sauce
1 teaspoon sugar
1/2 teaspoon salt
1/2 teaspoon ground black pepper
1 tablespoon rice flour or
  dry breadcrumbs
2 pounds fat rice noodles or rice
  vermicelli cooked al dente, strained,

and then rinsed in cool water
1/3 cup chopped cilantro or
  Vietnamese coriander
1 white onion, peeled and thinly sliced
3 scallions, thinly sliced on the bias
2 tablespoons vegetable oil

GARNISHES
Lime wedges
Fresh mint, Vietnamese coriander,
  cilantro, Asian basil (as available)
Lettuce or cabbage, sliced
  into thin strips
Bean sprouts (optional)
Thinly sliced serrano or Thai chiles
Chile sauce
Pickled garlic and chiles

◌ SERVES 8 ◌

ALTHOUGH THE TITLE of this dish, Bun Bo, implies that it is made with only beef, it actually contains pork and sometimes pork meatballs as well. Similar to Pho and served throughout the country, this meal-in-a-bowl soup is usually made with fat round noodles, and is a bit spicier and heartier with its characteristic, tiny reddish droplets of annatto and chile-tinged meat fat floating on the surface. This dish requires both a spoon and a set of chopsticks to enjoy its many com-ponents. The meatballs are optional, but they add another texture and flavor dimension. If you choose to omit them, you may want to use a bit more beef and pork.

I Place the beef bones, pork leg, and beef shank or brisket in a large pot and cover with cold water.

continued on page 108

Bring the water to a boil and cook for 5 minutes. Remove from the heat, drain immediately, and then rinse the meat and bones in cool water; drain and set aside. Clean the pot thoroughly.

2 Preheat the pot, add all but 2 tablespoons of the oil and then the onion, and cook for about 1 minute. Add the annatto seeds and stir until a nice amount of color is released. Season the beef and pork with salt and pepper, and brown slightly in the oil. Add the water, bring to a boil, lower the heat, and skim the surface for any scum that has accumulated. Lightly crush 3 of the lemongrass stalks, cut them into 2-inch segments, and add them to the stock along with 3 tablespoons fish sauce. Simmer for 1 hour and 15 minutes.

3 Remove the pork leg from the broth and immerse in cold water for 10 minutes to cool and preserve the color; drain and set aside. Continue simmering the broth for another hour. Remove the beef from the pot and immerse in cold water for 10 minutes to cool and preserve the color; drain and set aside.

4 Chop the remaining lemongrass finely and gently heat in the remaining oil along with the shallot, garlic, and chile flakes for about 5 minutes. Add this to the broth along with the shrimp sauce, if using, remaining fish sauce, and sugar. Simmer for 15–20 minutes more and turn off the heat; after about 20 minutes, skim off any excess fat on the surface of the broth. Strain and reheat when ready to serve.

5 In the meantime, mix together all of the meatball ingredients except the oil and form into 1-inch balls. Heat the oil in a deep skillet and lightly brown the meatballs. Add about 3 cups of the finished broth to the skillet and bring to a low boil, reduce to simmer for 15 minutes, and then remove the meatballs. (The broth may be strained through a cheesecloth and returned to the main pot after cooking the meatballs.)

6 Remove the excess fat and skin from the pork leg, then cut the pork and the beef into thin bite-size slices.

7 Reheat the noodles in a pot of boiling water and place a portion in each bowl. Heat the meat slices and the meatballs by dipping them in the hot broth using a strainer. Place some of the meat slices and several meatballs on top of the noodles, then add some of the herbs, onion, and scallions to each bowl. Ladle about 1½ to 2 cups of broth in each bowl and serve immediately, along with the garnishes.

The food of Vietnam reflects the history, climate, and geography of the country as well as the spirit of the populace.

SOUR SOUP WITH FISH
[CANH CA CHUA]

1½–2 pounds fresh fish fillets (catfish, bass, snapper, halibut, grouper, etc.), cut into 1-inch chunks
3 tablespoons fish sauce, divided
1 large or 2 medium shallots, minced
8 cups fish stock, chicken stock, or water
1 ounce tamarind pulp, dissolved in ½ cup boiling water and strained (reserve water)

1 clove garlic, sliced
2 stalks lemongrass, peeled, lightly crushed, and cut into 2-inch sections
2 teaspoons sugar
½ teaspoon salt
6 ounces cooked baby shrimp
1 cup diced pineapple
1–2 red serrano or Thai chiles, sliced
½ red bell pepper, seeded and cut into 1-inch pieces

2–3 okra pods, stems removed and sliced into quarters lengthwise
1 tomato, sliced into 8 wedges
2 scallions, sliced into 1-inch pieces diagonally
⅓ cup mixed cilantro and mint leaves, coarsely chopped
Lime wedges

☞ SERVES 4–5 AS A MAIN DISH OR 6–8 AS PART OF A LARGER MEAL ☜

SOUR SOUPS ARE often part of a multicourse Vietnamese meal on special occasions, but they are also hearty enough to serve as a lunch or light supper entree. My friend Khai Dzoan, chef at his mother's Cam Van Dzoan restaurant in Saigon, taught me this recipe. Not really that sour but tangy from tamarind, the soup is loaded with flavors from pineapple, chiles, lemongrass, herbs, shrimp, and fresh fish. Khai's recipe also called for taro stem, but I have omitted that, as it is a difficult find in the West. Serve with steamed rice or add noodles for a full meal.

I Marinate the fish pieces in 1 tablespoon of the fish sauce and the shallots. Place the stock in a large pot with the tamarind water, garlic, lemongrass, sugar, remaining fish sauce, and salt. Bring to a boil and cook for 10 minutes. Remove the lemongrass. Add the fish, shrimp, pineapple, chiles, bell pepper, and okra, and simmer for about 10–12 minutes, or until the fish is almost done. Add the tomato and scallions, and simmer another 5 minutes. Ladle into bowls and garnish with the herbs and lime wedges.

Beef in Vietnam, another meat that plays an important role in the cuisine of that country, is usually grass-fed with the distinctive flavor that comes with that sort of feeding. Grass-fed beef is usually not as tender, especially since it is not typically aged, so most Vietnamese recipes for beef call for it to be thinly sliced before or after it is cooked to make it easier to chew. For the most authentic taste, look for grass-fed beef where you can, but grain-fed varieties will also work fine.

BEEF
DISHES

THE RECIPES

VIETNAMESE BEEF STEW WITH STAR ANISE AND BASIL

[BO KHO]

---

1 tablespoon ground annatto seeds (achiote) or mild paprika

2 teaspoons Chinese five-spice powder, or 1 teaspoon curry powder and ½ teaspoon ground cinnamon

1 tablespoon raw or brown sugar

½ teaspoon salt

½ teaspoon freshly ground white or black pepper

2–2½ pounds boneless beef chuck or beef stew meat, cut into 1½-inch cubes

3 tablespoons vegetable oil

2 tablespoons minced fresh ginger

3–4 cloves garlic, minced

2 tablespoons chopped shallots or scallions

½ cup seeded and finely diced tomatoes, or ⅓ cup tomato puree

3½ cups beef broth, chicken broth, or water

2 tablespoons fish sauce (Vietnamese is preferred)

2 tablespoons soy sauce

6–8 (3-inch) pieces lemongrass, lightly crushed; if not available,

add 2 tablespoons lime juice at the end of cooking

1 or 2 red serrano or jalapeño chiles, chopped; or 1–2 teaspoons hot chile flakes

3–4 whole star anise, lightly toasted

½ pound carrots, peeled and cut into ½-inch-thick rounds

½ cup coarsely chopped Asian basil leaves

½ cup very thinly sliced onion

¼ cup whole cilantro leaves

☞ SERVES 6 ☜

THIS FAIRLY SIMPLE recipe is a great example of Vietnamese comfort food. Often served steaming hot at breakfast along with crusty, freshly baked baguette, Bo Kho also makes a great dinner for a cold winter's night when served over noodles or steamed jasmine rice. The rich gravy-like broth is satisfying, and the aromatic star anise, basil, cilantro, and lemongrass give it a faintly exotic aroma and that characteristic Vietnamese fresh quality. Sometimes potatoes are added along with the carrots and, in the south, whole eggs are often simmered in the stew during the last few minutes of cooking. This is a one-pot dish that is traditionally cooked in terra-cotta pots, but any heavy skillet, large pot, or Dutch oven that you have will work just fine.

I Mix the annatto, five-spice powder, sugar, salt, and pepper together; toss with the beef.

continued on page 120

2 Heat the oil to very hot in a heavy skillet or pot and brown the meat well. Add the ginger, garlic, and shallots, and continue cooking for 1–2 minutes. Add the tomato and stir-fry for 2 minutes more while stirring.

3 Pour in the broth; add the fish sauce, soy sauce, lemongrass, chiles, and star anise. Bring to a boil and reduce to a high simmer.

4 Cook for 40–60 minutes, stirring occasionally, until the meat is fork-tender. Add the carrots and cook for 15 minutes more, or until tender. The liquid should have a light gravy-like consistency. Taste for salt and add more fish or soy sauce if needed. Remove the lemongrass, if desired, and stir in the basil. Serve topped with onion and cilantro.

Sliced Beef with Asparagus
[Thit Bo Mang Tay]

1 tablespoon soy sauce	12 ounces beef, chuck, sirloin,	2 teaspoons minced shallots
1 teaspoon fish sauce	or round steak, thinly sliced	1 pound asparagus, woody stem
1 tablespoon rice wine or dry sherry	and cut into bite-size pieces	ends removed and the remaining
1 teaspoon sugar	3 tablespoons vegetable oil	tender part cut into 1-inch sections
¼ teaspoon ground black pepper	1 (1-inch) piece ginger, peeled and	1 tablespoon oyster sauce
1 tablespoon cornstarch	sliced into 3 smaller pieces	1 tablespoon beef both,
	2 cloves garlic, peeled and sliced	chicken broth, or water

⊛ SERVES 2 AS A MAIN DISH OR 4–6 AS PART OF A LARGER MEAL ⊛

A CHINESE-STYLE DISH with French-introduced asparagus, this is a true fusion food. I had this at a small restaurant in Hue, and it was simply delicious. Some other vegetables like broccoli or green beans could be substituted here. Serve it with jasmine rice or some noodles.

I Mix the soy sauce, fish sauce, rice wine, sugar, pepper, and cornstarch in a bowl until smooth. Mix in the beef slices until well coated and marinate 15 minutes.

2 Heat the oil in a wok. Add the ginger, garlic, shallots, and asparagus. Stir-fry for 1–2 minutes, or until the asparagus is warmed through and tender with a little color around the edges. Remove from the wok with a slotted spoon and reserve.

3 Add the beef to the pan and spread it around the surface of the wok so that all of the pieces have contact with the oil. Stir-fry for 2–3 minutes, or until the beef is cooked through. Add the reserved asparagus and ginger mixtures, and cook 30 seconds to warm through. Add the oyster sauce and broth, and stir well to coat. Remove from the wok and serve.

THE PEOPLE
AND FLAVORS OF
HO CHI MINH

Everyone in Ho Chi Minh City, or Saigon, as most locals and visitors call it, seems to be in business for themselves. Street vendors hawk food, drink, tourist trinkets, fruits and vegetables, clothes, jewelry, books, music, and electronics. Many homes double as businesses, with the street front access used as a café, restaurant, pharmacy, laundry, travel agency, office, mini mart, copy shop, clothing store, or whatever else they deem may be of interest to others.

The food in Saigon is nothing short of marvelous. It seems that everywhere you turn, there is a food option. Cafes, traditional restaurants, elegant French restaurants, bakeries, and modern "fusion" establishments seem to be on each block. On top of that, there are countless operators on the sidewalks, offering Pho, Banh Xeo, coffee and tea, smoothies (a Saigon specialty), soups, grilled meats, and seafood. Each evening, one street-side eatery has nearly 200 people sitting at small plastic tables and stools on one side of the street, with the kitchen on the other—all on the sidewalk. The fresh seafood that they specialize in is live in a tank just before cooking, and the quality and flavors

are astounding. Other restaurant favorites in Ho Chi Minh City are the ones that cater to large groups of Vietnamese locals and seem to be the choice for birthday and other special occasion get-togethers. They seat hundreds and are gaudily arrayed with Chinese artifacts and neon lighting. They often specialize in char-grilled items and frequently have grill-at-the-

table dishes on the menu. When dining at these establishments, your nose will be enticed by exotic aromas and your ears assaulted by loud music, the popping of wet towel bags, the strains of "Happy Birthday" sung in English, and the traditional Vietnamese toast of "Mot, Hai, Bac (1, 2, 3)!"

STIR-FRIED BEEF WITH CRISPY FRIED POTATOES

[KHOAI TAY CHIEN XAO THIT BO]

3 quarts water

2 teaspoons salt

1½ pounds potatoes (white, red rose, Yukon gold, or russet)

1 tablespoon fish sauce

1 teaspoon hoisin or soy sauce

1 teaspoon sugar

½ teaspoon ground black pepper

1½ teaspoons cornstarch, or 1 teaspoon arrowroot

1 shallot, peeled and minced

1 teaspoon minced ginger

1 clove garlic, minced

1¼ pounds beef sirloin, chuck, strip, flank, or other steak, sliced about ⅛ to ¼ inch thick across the grain and then cut into bite-size pieces

1–2 cups vegetable oil (depending on the pan used for frying), divided

1 cup beef broth or water

2 tablespoons chopped cilantro (optional)

1–2 scallions, cut into 2-inch segments and then finely julienned

∾ SERVES 3–4 AS A MAIN DISH OR 5–8 AS PART OF A LARGER MEAL ∾

THE FRENCH INFLUENCE is still evident in Vietnamese cooking, albeit filtered through Vietnamese style and practicality. This dish is a fine example of that influence, likely originating with the classic French dish, *bifteck frites*. Many versions of this can be enjoyed at cafes, small restaurants, and even at street vendor stalls; sometimes it is as simple as a piece of beefsteak that is sauced with gravy along with some basic french fries, and often served with a salad of lettuce, cucumbers, and tomatoes on the side. This recipe is a stir-fry that almost makes its own gravy and has the distinctive Vietnamese flavor of fish sauce and cilantro with a touch of ginger. I use a waffle-cut potato slice produced by using a mandoline, as it gives the crispi-

est results. On the crinkle-slice blade, first slice a thin piece of potato and discard it, then rotate the potato 90 degrees and slice, this will form the waffle cut. Continue rotating after each slice. Regular thin slices will also work fine as well a more typical "french fry" cut. After slicing, keep the potatoes in very cold water to help them stay crisp and to prevent discoloration. This stir-fry could also be served with noodles or rice instead of potatoes.

I Bring the water and salt to a boil, then blanch the potatoes in 3–4 batches for 2–3 minutes; immediately rinse in cold water to cool completely, then drain.

continued on page 128

2 Mix the fish sauce, hoisin, sugar, pepper, and cornstarch together until smooth. Stir in the shallot, ginger, and garlic. Mix well with the beef slices until all of the surfaces of the meat are coated well.

3 Place 2–3 inches oil in a pan that is at least 5 inches deep. Heat the oil to 350–365 degrees, or until a few wisps of smoke rise from the surface.

4 Thoroughly blot the potatoes dry with a cloth or paper towel. Fry the potatoes in 2–3 batches until golden brown; drain on paper towels.

5 Heat 2–3 tablespoons oil in a wok on high heat and add the marinated beef. Stir briefly to spread the slices evenly around on the surface of the wok and let cook until they begin to brown a bit, about 1–1½ minutes. Stir and continue cooking for about 3–4 minutes more, add the broth, and bring to a boil, cooking until the "gravy" has thickened. Taste for salt and adjust if needed, then stir in the cilantro. Serve the beef and sauce over the crispy potatoes and garnish with the scallions.

BEEF GRILLED IN WILD PEPPER LEAVES

[BO NUONG LA LOT]

12 ounces ground beef	1 tablespoon fish sauce	1 teaspoon yellow curry
2 tablespoons finely	1 teaspoon sugar	powder or dry turmeric
minced lemongrass	2 teaspoons hoisin or oyster sauce	30–36 La Lot leaves, rinsed and wiped
2 tablespoons finely minced shallots	½ teaspoon ground pepper	dry (found in Asian markets)
2 cloves garlic, finely minced		2 tablespoons vegetable oil

∽ SERVES 3–4 ∽

THE WILD PEPPER leaf, *piper sarmentosum*, sometimes called betel leak but not related to the common betel, is used to season some dishes in Vietnamese cooking but is more often used to wrap meats for cooking, as in this recipe. There is not much aroma to this leaf until it is cooked, when it releases its peppery herbal flavor. Bo Nuong La Lot is a snack or appetizer item, but when combined with some steamed rice and vegetables, it makes a nice meal. Some of the best places to get Bo Nuong La Lot are at street stands and in the markets, particularly in Saigon. Serve with lettuce and herbs to wrap them or with rice or noodles and some Basic Vietnamese Dipping Sauce (page 42).

1 Mix the ground beef with the lemongrass, shallots, garlic, fish sauce, sugar, hoisin, pepper, and curry powder; combine well and let sit for about 30 minutes. Soak 12 bamboo skewers in hot water for 30 minutes; set aside.

2 Lay a La Lot leaf on the counter and center a heaping tablespoon of the meat mixture on the lower third of the leaf. Fold the bottom edge over the filling, and then fold the left and right edges of the leaf to overlap the bottom flap. Roll to form a tight cylinder and set aside; repeat until all of the filling is used.

3 Lay 6 of the rolled cylinders next to each other and slide one skewer through all of the rolls towards one end. Then slide another skewer through the other end. Repeat with the remaining rolls.

4 Preheat a grill to medium. Brush the leaves wrapping the beef with a little of the oil and then place on the grill. Cook slowly, turning occasionally, until the beef is rendering some fat and the leaves are slightly charred, about 6–7 minutes. Remove from the heat, let rest a few minutes, remove the skewers, and serve.

GRILLED BEEF WITH OKRA, TOMATOES, AND PINEAPPLE
[BO NUONG]

1½ pounds beef sirloin, chuck, or top round, thinly sliced across the grain in about 1 x 2½-inch pieces
Marinade for Grilled Meats (page 47)
3 tablespoons vegetable oil
1 shallot, minced
2 cloves garlic, minced

½ teaspoon salt
½ teaspoon black pepper
2–3 medium tomatoes, each sliced into 8 wedges
1 medium white onion, cut into 8 wedges

10–12 scallions, root ends

removed and tops trimmed to about 4–5 inches in length
½ small-to-medium pineapple, skinned, cored, and sliced across into ¼-inch-thick slices
6–8 large okra pods, stemmed and cut in half lengthwise

∽ SERVES 4–5 ∽

MANY VERSIONS OF this dish exist with a number of variations around the country. All are cooked at the table by the diners; some places have you cook the meat and vegetables on a skillet or pan that is placed over burning coals or a sterno-like parafin burner, and others use a grate for a true char-grilled flavor. Either way is a lot of fun and provides an interactive social experience along with the tasty meal. I based this recipe on two restaurants: an unnamed tiny operation on Ma May Street in Hanoi's old quarter, and Lac Canh in the beach resort of Nha Trang. The meat is marinated ahead of time; the vegetables and the fruit are lightly coated with shallot-and-garlic-scented oil. The diners then begin to cook some of everything and start eating as items are done. It is a community effort with plenty of flashing chopsticks in play. If you are not set up to have the guests participate in the cooking, it is still a worthy dish to present at the table already plated.

1 Mix the meat with the marinade and set aside for 20–30 minutes.

2 Combine the oil with the shallot, garlic, salt, and pepper, and lightly brush the mixture over the tomatoes, onion, scallions, pineapple slices, and okra.

3 Cook the meat slices, vegetables, and fruit on a charcoal or gas grill or on a stovetop grill until done. Serve immediately.

Pork is very popular for Vietnamese cooking, probably a legacy from the Chinese and reinforced during the French Colonial period. Most families that live in the countryside try to raise at least a few pigs, from the small, pot-bellied, black varieties of the far north to the larger, fatter, white breeds seen often in the Mekong Delta. This animal provides the meat and byproducts for both everyday meals and special-occasion fare.

PORK
DISHES

THE RECIPES

GRILLED FIVE-SPICE PORK CHOPS
[THIT HEO NUONG NGU VI HUONG]

MARINADE
2 tablespoons minced shallot
8 cloves garlic, minced
2 tablespoons fish sauce

1 tablespoon soy sauce
2 teaspoons sugar
1½ teaspoons five-spice powder
½ teaspoon black pepper

2 tablespoons lime juice
3 tablespoons vegetable oil

4–6 (¾- to 1-inch-thick) pork chops

☙ SERVES 4–6 AS PART OF A LARGER MEAL ❧

THIS SIMPLE YET delicious dish is a staple at many inexpensive restaurants. Usually served with a soup, rice, and vegetables or salad, it makes for a nice lunch or supper. To avoid drying out the meat, choose thick, bone-in rib chops, as they have a bit more fat than the loin chops, and the bone helps keep them moist and adds flavor too. The chops can be served whole, eaten with a knife and fork, or sliced before bringing to the table so that they can be handled with chopsticks. Leftovers are great for fried rice or in sandwiches. Serve with Basic Vietnamese Dipping Sauce (page 42) and/or Salt, Pepper and Lime Dipping Sauce (page 33).

1 Combine all of the marinade ingredients and let sit for a few minutes. Place the pork chops in a nonreactive dish and cover them with the marinade, making sure all of the meat has been coated; cover and marinate for 1–3 hours or overnight.

NOTE: If you marinate for more than 1 hour, you need to refrigerate the chops and then remove from the refrigerator 30–45 minutes before grilling.

2 Preheat a charcoal or gas grill and cook the chops about 4–6 minutes on the first side and 3–4 minutes on the second, being careful not to overcook. Rest a few minutes and serve whole or sliced.

The aspects of flavor, aroma, texture, color, contrast, balance, and even the sound a food makes are all taken into consideration in the planning and creation of a Vietnamese meal.

Stir-Fried Pork with Baby Bok Choy
[Thit Heo Xao Cai Be Trang]

2 tablespoons fish sauce	½ teaspoon salt	3 tablespoons vegetable oil, divided
2 cloves garlic, minced	¼ teaspoon black pepper	1 pound baby bok choy, cut in
1 teaspoon finely minced lemongrass	1 tablespoon lime juice	half lengthwise or in quarters
½ teaspoon chile paste, or ¼	1½ pounds pork shoulder, loin,	(depending on the size)
teaspoon dry chile flakes	or leg meat, thinly sliced and	1 white onion, peeled and cut
2 teaspoons sugar	cut into bite-size pieces	into bite-size chunks

∽ SERVES 2–3 AS A MAIN DISH OR 4–6 AS PART OF A LARGER MEAL ∽

THIS IS A simple stir-fry that uses basic Vietnamese flavors and would usually be part of a multicourse meal. The bok choy could easily be replaced with broccoli, cauliflower, or other vegetables. The natural sweet and slightly bitter taste of the bok choy contrasts nicely with the rich saltiness of the pork. This dish is typical of Vietnamese stir-fries in that a minimal amount of oil is used and the natural moisture of the ingredients along with the marinade is all of the sauce that is added to the dish. Serve it with Basic Vietnamese Dipping Sauce (page 42).

1 Mix together the fish sauce, garlic, lemongrass, chile paste, sugar, salt, pepper, and lime juice; add the sliced pork and marinate for 20–30 minutes.

2 Heat 2 tablespoons oil in a wok until very hot. Stir-fry the bok choy and onion briefly to set the color and brown the onions slightly around the edges. Remove the vegetables from the wok with tongs and reserve. Add the remaining oil to the wok, and when it just begins to smoke, add the pork and spread it evenly around the surface of the wok to sear. When a bit of color develops around the edges of the pork, stir it briefly, fry for 30 seconds more, and add the vegetables back into the wok. Stir again several times until the meat is cooked through and the vegetables have thrown off a little moisture. Remove from the wok and serve immediately.

GRILLED PORK SPARE RIBS
[SUON NUONG]

6 to 6½ pounds pork spareribs,
  back membrane removed and
  separated into individual ribs
  (about 2 racks; have your butcher
  split into riblets if desired)
1 white onion, peeled and quartered
4 cloves garlic, peeled and crushed
2 stalks lemongrass, lightly crushed
  and cut into 2-inch sections
½ teaspoon whole black peppercorns
½ teaspoon salt

1 (1-inch) piece ginger, peeled and
  sliced into 3 smaller pieces (optional)
3 star anise (optional)

MARINADE
4 tablespoons Caramel
  Sauce (page 40)
2 tablespoons raw or brown sugar
2 tablespoons fish sauce
3 tablespoons soy sauce
1 tablespoon hoisin sauce

2 tablespoons rice or
  distilled white vinegar
2–3 teaspoons chile garlic paste, or
  1 teaspoon dry chile flakes crushed
  together with 4 cloves garlic
2 shallots, peeled and minced
¼ cup thinly sliced lemongrass,
  crushed in a mortar and pestle
¼ cup finely chopped cilantro
2 tablespoons vegetable oil

SERVES 8–10 AS AN APPETIZER, 3–5 AS A MAIN DISH, OR 6–8 AS PART OF A LARGER MEAL

WHEN I COOK these ribs, I always wish that I had made more, as they disappear quickly; it is wonderful to have leftovers, so I have called for a lot of ribs here. This recipe is derived from street-vendor and small-restaurant styles combined with some of the tricks that I have learned about grilling over the years. I often find that the typical Vietnamese method of marinating raw ribs and then going directly to the charcoal grill, although it produces tasty results, also often makes for chewy ribs, and the marinade can easily burn while trying to cook the meat sufficiently. I parboil the ribs to cook them through before marinating, yielding flavorful and tender results. That step may be done a day or two ahead of time. If you are set up for slow, even-heated char grilling or smoking, you can skip the boiling step and cook the ribs for 2–2½ hours. If you prefer not to deal with the bones, you could also use boneless country-style ribs and then slice them before serving.

I Place the ribs, onion, garlic, lemongrass, peppercorns, salt, ginger, and star anise into a large pot and cover with cool water, about 3–4 quarts. Bring to a boil and then reduce to a low boil and cook,

continued on page 144

uncovered, for 45 minutes to 1 hour, or until the meat is beginning to get tender. Turn off the heat, let sit for 15 minutes, and then drain; separate the ribs from the rest of the seasonings and then discard the seasonings.

2 Mix together all of the marinade ingredients and then toss with the ribs. Cover and marinate in the refrigerator for at least 2 hours or overnight. Stir the ribs several times during marinating to evenly distribute the flavors.

3 Preheat a char-grill to medium-low or medium heat. Carefully remove the ribs from the marinade so that you will have some marinade to use later in the cooking process. Begin cooking the ribs, turning occasionally as color develops to prevent burning. After about 10 minutes, brush the ribs with some of the marinade. Cook 5–7 minutes more and then brush one more time. Discard the remaining marinade and cook the ribs a final 7–10 minutes more, or until the marinade has caramelized on the meat and there is some charring around the edges.

HUE MINCED PORK PATTIES
[THIT HEO NEM XAO]

2 teaspoons Chile-Garlic-Oil Table Condiment (page 44); 2 teaspoons commercial chile-garlic paste; or 1 teaspoon dried chile flakes smashed together with 5 cloves garlic
1 cup coarsely chopped raw shrimp

8 ounces ground pork
½ cup thinly sliced, and very finely minced lemongrass
2 tablespoons + 1 teaspoon sugar
2 tablespoons + 1 teaspoon fish sauce
⅓ cup water

1 tablespoon shrimp sauce
4 tablespoons vegetable oil
¼ cup chopped toasted peanuts
1 scallion, thinly sliced into rings

☞ SERVES 6–8 AS AN APPETIZER OR 4–6 AS PART OF A LARGER MEAL ☜

IN THIS DISH from central Vietnam, the meat is often cooked loose, and the caramelized salty pieces are mixed with copious amounts of rice; however, at the suggestion of Madam Huy, my chef friend and well-known Hue Imperial cuisine expert, I form the meat into small patties, a more elegant presentation in keeping with the style of the royal court. With the addition of shrimp sauce, this dish is quite strongly flavored, and for Western tastes, it is probably better suited when served as an appetizer or along with other less bold dishes.

1 Mix together the chile-garlic paste, shrimp, pork, lemongrass, 1 teaspoon sugar, and 1 teaspoon fish sauce; form into patties, about ⅓ inch thick and 2 inches in diameter. Mix together the water, shrimp sauce, remaining sugar and fish sauce; set aside.

2 Heat the oil in a large flat-bottomed skillet and brown the patties on both sides. Add the shrimp sauce mixture and cook about 3–4 minutes; then turn the patties over and continue cooking until most of the liquid has evaporated and caramelized around the edges of the patties. NOTE: You may need to reduce the heat as the liquid evaporates to prevent burning.

3 Remove the patties to a serving plate and garnish with the peanuts and scallion.

In general, Vietnamese cook-ing is a tantalizing blend of clean, fresh, bright, sweet, and hot flavors. Steaming, stewing, and grilling techniques are more common than frying. Fresh herbs and hot chiles play an important role.

CARAMELIZED AND STEAMED PORK FOR TET

[KHAU NHUC]

2 tablespoons pork lard or vegetable oil	½ cup Caramel Sauce (page 40)	2 teaspoons five-spice powder
2½–3 pounds boneless pork shoulder roast, cut into 2 or 3 chunks	1 white onion, peeled and chopped	½ teaspoon salt
	4 cloves garlic, peeled and minced	¼ cup brewed green tea or water
	2 tablespoons fish sauce	Banana leaves

∽ SERVES 4–5 AS A MAIN DISH OR 6–8 AS PART OF A LARGER MEAL ∽

ON MY SECOND trip to Vietnam, I returned to the far north to the mountain village of Sa Pa. My guide friend, Miss Moon (Min Hang Nha), took me to cook with a family there. It was the week before Tet, the lunar New Year celebration, and the man of the house was well known for his special-occasion cooking. He helped me to cook this dish in his kitchen, which is traditionally prepared for the Tet holiday. The stove was a grate made from reinforcement bars on the floor, all fueled by bamboo sticks. This method requires some extended cooking time, but you can shortcut it a bit by finishing the pork in the oven instead of the steamer. Instead of wrapping it in banana leaves, place it in a roasting pan along with ½ cup of extra water, seal tightly, and bake for 2½ hours at 350 degrees. His recipe uses dried kale, a local product with a slightly bitter homemade ingredient that I have been unable to find at home. I use some stir-fried or steamed cabbage or kale served on the side instead. If you are using the oven method, you could add the raw greens to the roasting pork for the last 30 minutes to mingle the flavors with the meat.

∽

I In a heavy skillet or wok, heat the lard or oil until very hot. Sear the pork in the fat until well-browned on all surfaces. Remove the pan from the heat and pour in the Caramel Sauce (beware of hot splatters). When the sauce has calmed down a bit, return the pan to the heat and continue cooking until the Caramel Sauce forms a thick coating on the surface of the meat.

2 Mix the onion, garlic, fish sauce, five-spice powder, salt, and tea together; set aside.

3 Briefly toast the banana leaves directly over the heat to make them flexible. Tear off a few strips to use as a tie and lay out the leaves, 2 layers thick, then place the meat in the center. Pour the seasonings over the meat and make sure they are evenly distributed. Wrap the banana leaves around the meat to make a closed package and secure with banana leaf ties. Place in a steamer and steam on low for 5 hours. Carefully remove a package, open, and check for doneness. The meat should be fork-tender. Cut into bite-size pieces and serve.

Poultry, especially chicken, is a high-end protein in Vietnam. Chicken is more expensive than most seafood and is used for special occasions. A family that can afford chicken is deemed prosperous by many standards. Almost the entire animal is utilized. Other birds, like duck, goose, quail, and a number of smaller species, also figure in the recipes of Vietnam. Most birds in Vietnam are not killed until near the time to cook them, and frozen chicken is almost unheard of, so freshness is very important when choosing poultry for Vietnamese dishes.

POULTRY DISHES

THE RECIPES

"Chicken Street" Lemongrass and Chile Grilled Chicken
[Ga Nuong]

2 large boneless, skinless chicken breasts or thighs 2 medium stalks lemongrass, crushed and very finely chopped	2–3 cloves garlic, finely chopped 2 teaspoons raw or light brown sugar 2 teaspoons light soy sauce 2 teaspoons fish sauce	1 or 2 serrano or jalapeño chiles, stemmed, seeded, and finely minced 1/4 teaspoon ground white pepper 1/2 lime, juiced 2 tablespoons vegetable oil

∽ SERVES 4 ∽

THIS RECIPE RE-CREATES the flavors of Hanoi grilled chicken with a little influence from another spot in Saigon that I was shown by my chef friend Khai. I have used boneless breast or thighs to make the dish a little more elegant; however, the spicy marinade will work fine for all parts of the bird, bone in or not, and I have also used it successfully on a whole bird that I split open on the back side and slow-grilled to perfection. This chicken is also very good when served cold, perfect for a picnic, and the leftovers can be used for a chicken salad or fried rice.

1 Butterfly the chicken by slitting each breast horizontally so that it is still joined on one side and then open it up.

2 Place on a cutting board or flat countertop, cover it with plastic wrap, and then gently pound to an even thickness with a meat mallet or a rolling pin.

3 Combine the remaining ingredients in a bowl, mix thoroughly, and then coat the chicken. Cover and let marinate for at least 1 hour. Place the chicken on a hot char grill and cook about 3–4 minutes on each side, or until cooked through. Slice and serve with mint leaves, Asian basil or cilantro, cucumber slices, and steamed jasmine rice, if desired.

CLAY-POT GINGERED CHICKEN
[GA KHO GUNG]

1 whole fryer chicken, cut-up fryer, or 8 chicken thighs	3 inches gingerroot, peeled and sliced	2 tablespoons Caramel Sauce (page 40)
3 tablespoons vegetable oil	4 cloves garlic, minced	3 scallions, cut into 1½- to 2-inch lengths
Salt and pepper	1 teaspoon sugar	
1 large or 2 medium shallots, peeled and sliced	2 tablespoons fish sauce	⅛ cup cilantro leaves
	1–2 serrano or Thai chiles, sliced	
	1 cup chicken broth	

⌒ SERVES 4–6 AS A MAIN DISH OR 6–8 AS PART OF A LARGER MEAL ⌒

DISHES THAT ARE braised in a clay pot are usually identified by the word Kho. They often use Caramel Sauce to help make them rich in flavor. These types of dishes originate in the countryside where cooks, using a simple array of ingredients, coax out the maximum flavor through clever techniques. If you do not have a clay pot, a covered heavy casserole or Dutch oven will also work fine. Serve clay-pot dishes with steamed rice, a vegetable or two, and/or a salad.

I Rinse the chicken and pat dry. If using a whole chicken, cut into leg, thigh, wing, and breast sections. Cut each section (except the wings) in half again through the bone. You can remove the skin or leave it on, as you prefer.

2 Heat a clay pot or Dutch oven on high and add the oil. Season the chicken with salt and pepper and then brown in the oil; remove from the pot and set aside.

3 Add the shallots and ginger to the hot oil and sauté briefly. Stir in the garlic, sugar, fish sauce, chiles, and browned chicken. Stir several times and then add the broth and Caramel Sauce. Bring to a boil, cover, reduce the heat to simmer, and cook for 20 minutes. Uncover, stir, and continue cooking about 15 minutes more. Stir in the scallions, remove from the heat, and let sit for 5 minutes before serving. Garnish with cilantro leaves.

CHICKEN AND SWEET POTATO CURRY

[CA RI GA KHOAI LANG]

2–3 stalks lemongrass, trimmed, halved lengthwise, and finely minced

2 shallots or 1 white onion, peeled and coarsely chopped

3 cloves garlic, chopped

1–2 red serrano or Thai chiles or ½–1 teaspoon dry chile flakes

1 inch galangal or ginger, peeled and chopped

3 tablespoons vegetable oil

2½–3 pounds bone-in chicken thighs and/or legs (skin removed or not, as you prefer)

Salt and pepper

2 tablespoons Vietnamese yellow curry powder or Madras curry powder

1 teaspoon dry turmeric

3 tablespoons fish sauce

2 teaspoons sugar

¼ cup chicken broth or water

1¾ cups unsweetened coconut milk (1 [13-ounce] can)

1½ pounds sweet potato, peeled and cut into 1-inch chunks (to prevent browning, store in cool water until ready to use)

½ cup mixed Asian basil and cilantro leaves

½ cup thinly sliced onion or scallions

☞ SERVES 4–6 ☜

POPULAR IN SAIGON at street stalls and markets, and in small restaurants as well as at home, Vietnamese curries are a bit lighter than Indian-style recipes and carry the distinctive Vietnamese flavor combination of lemongrass and fish sauce. The sweet potatoes may be replaced with potatoes and/or carrots if you like. This hearty dish is typically served with baguettes or steamed rice. Steamed vegetables or a salad go well with this dish as well.

I Smash the lemongrass, shallots, garlic, chiles, and galangal in a mortar and pestle, one ingredient at a time, until a paste is formed; or use a food processor.

2 Heat the oil in a heavy pot or deep skillet and season the chicken with salt and pepper; add chicken to the pot, brown on all sides, and then remove.

3 Add the lemongrass paste, curry powder, and turmeric to the hot oil and stir, cooking to release the fragrant flavors. Return the chicken to the pan and add the fish sauce, sugar, broth, and coconut milk; bring to a boil, then reduce the heat to simmer. Cook for 15 minutes and then add the sweet potatoes. Cook 15–20 minutes more, or until the potatoes are tender. Turn off the heat and let sit for 15 minutes so the flavors combine. Transfer to a serving dish and garnish with the herbs and onion.

THE PEOPLE AND FLAVORS OF THE MEKONG DELTA

K nown as the River of the Nine Dragons because of the nine main branches that it has split into before reaching the sea, the Mekong River has its origins in the highlands of Tibet and passes through China, Myanmar, Thailand, Laos, and Cambodia on its more than 2,800-mile journey to Vietnam. In addition to the nine main branches, there are hundreds, if not thousands, of smaller waterways and canals that crisscross the delta, providing life-giving water and transportation. The rich soil created from the silt and dirt carried downstream is ideal for a diversity of crops. Rice is number one, closely followed by coconuts and a wide assortment of fruits. Vegeta-

bles are also in profusion here, and it seems that there is no shortage of food. The annual income and the overall standard of living in the delta are, in fact, a bit above the other agricultural areas in the country, due to the ease of growing in this verdant region. The rice growers can produce three, sometimes four harvests each year, compared to one or two in the north.

This abundance of staple food products and fresh fruits and vegetables fuels a unique distribution system in the area. Floating markets are seen throughout the region, with the largest and most well-known near Can Tho, the principal and most prosperous city in the Mekong. These floating markets are a riot of color and a cacophony of sounds that begin the day well before dawn.

Although a few tourists do visit the float-ing markets, these are the real thing and have been around for hundreds of years, because water has always been a safer and more reliable form of transportation than over the jungle-covered land.

The food also shows the wide variety of prod-ucts in this area; with many fruits, the dishes tend to be a bit sweeter than in the north, and there is a con-

spicuous use of more spices and herbs than in many
parts of Vietnam. Many flavors and techniques have
traveled down the river from Thailand and Cambodia, and there is a large percentage of Khmer people

here, so the dishes are not as "pure Vietnamese" as
in other parts of the country.

Duck Stewed with Pineapple and Cilantro

[Vit Nau Dua (Thom)]

1 small to medium duck, trimmed and
   cut into 9–12 pieces (leave the bone in)
Salt and pepper

MARINADE
2 tablespoons minced shallots
4 cloves garlic, minced
1 tablespoon juice squeezed
   from gingerroot

2 tablespoons fish sauce
2 tablespoons soy sauce
¼ cup pineapple juice
1 teaspoon sugar
1 teaspoon five-spice powder
2 teaspoons toasted sesame oil
⅓ cup Asian basil leaves
3 tablespoons vegetable oil, divided
1 medium white onion, peeled
   and cut into 8 wedges

2 slices peeled gingerroot
½ cup chicken broth or water
1 small-to-medium pineapple,
   peeled, halved lengthwise, and
   cored (reserve the juice for
   the marinade and sauce)
2 teaspoons mild vinegar
½ cup cilantro leaves

☙ SERVES 4–6 ❧

LIKELY ANOTHER FRENCH legacy, with a hint of Chinese influence as well, this dish is more popular in the south, where pineapples are plentiful, although I have also seen it in Hue and Hanoi. The tart sweetness of the pineapple plays against the fatty richness of the duck meat. By using the fresh pineapple juice, you will have the tenderizing benefit of the natural enzymes present in the fruit. The pineapple slices are traditionally seared in a pan to caramelize them slightly, but I like cooking them on the char grill whenever possible to add the extra dimension of a subtle smoky flavor. Serve with steamed rice, sautéed potatoes, or rice noodles with fresh herbs, and crisp vegetables or a salad to provide contrast.

1 Season the duck with salt and pepper, and place in a nonreactive pan. Mix all of the marinade ingredients together and add to the duck. Mix well, cover, and refrigerate for at least 3 hours and up to overnight.

2 Heat 2 tablespoons oil in a heavy pan and cook the duck pieces slowly until much of the fat is rendered and the skin is browned nicely. NOTE: Cook skin-side down mostly to avoid overcooking the meat. Pour off any excess fat and then add the onion and ginger. Stir until the onion has a bit of color, and then add the chicken broth and any reserved pineapple juice. Bring to a boil, reduce to a simmer, and cook for 25–30 minutes, stirring occasionally.

3 Slice half of the pineapple across into ¼-inch-thick segments, juice, and strain the other half (yields about ¾ to 1 cup juice). Brush the pineapple slices with the remaining oil and char-grill or pan-sear to caramelize slightly; set aside. Do not overcook.

4 Add the vinegar and the pineapple slices to the pan and cook 10–12 minutes more, or until the duck is tender. Remove from heat, skim off any excess fat, remove the ginger, and stir in the cilantro leaves. Serve immediately.

GRILLED FIVE-SPICE CHICKEN
[GA NUONG NGU VI HUONG]

MARINADE

2 tablespoons minced shallot

2 tablespoons minced ginger

6 cloves garlic, minced

1 tablespoon fish sauce

2 tablespoons soy sauce

2 teaspoons sugar

1½ teaspoons five-spice powder

¼ cup chopped Asian basil leaves

½ teaspoon black pepper

2 tablespoons lime juice

3 tablespoons vegetable oil

2¼- to 2½-pound fryer chicken,
   cut into 8 or 9 pieces

⬠ SERVES 4–6 AS PART OF A LARGER MEAL ⬠

SIMILAR TO THE method for Five-Spice Pork Chops (page 136) with the addition of basil in the marinade, chicken requires a bit slower and longer cooking. You could also use boneless chicken breast, but I prefer the bone-in chicken for flavor. Serve this with steamed rice, veggies, and some Basic Vietnamese Dipping Sauce (page 42) and/or Salt, Pepper, and Lime Dipping Sauce (page 33).

1 Combine all of the marinade ingredients and let sit for a few minutes. Place the chicken pieces in a nonreactive dish and cover them with the marinade, making sure all of the meat has been coated. Cover and marinate for 1–3 hours.

NOTE: If you marinate for more than 1 hour, refrigerate the chops and then remove from the refrigerator 30 minutes before grilling.

2 Preheat a charcoal or gas grill to medium and cook chicken about 8–10 minutes on the first side and 6–8 minutes on the second, being careful not to burn. Rest a few minutes before serving.

Steamed Chicken with Mushrooms

[Nam Dong Co Tiem Ga]

1 inch peeled gingerroot, minced
½ teaspoon ground black pepper
1 tablespoon fish sauce or soy sauce
1 teaspoon toasted sesame
  oil (optional)
Dash of salt

2 cloves garlic, minced
1½ pounds boneless, skinless
  chicken breast and/or thighs,
  cut into bite-size pieces
6 ounces shiitake or other firm
  mushrooms, halved or quartered
  (about 6–8 good-size mushrooms)

2–3 scallions, cut diagonally
  into 1-inch segments
Chopped cilantro or Vietnamese
  coriander (optional)

❧ SERVES 4 AS A MAIN DISH OR 6–8 AS PART OF A LARGER MEAL ❧

SIMPLE STEAMED MEATS and vegetables are often the center point of family meals in Vietnam. Served with a dipping sauce and some rice, this type of meal is easy to prepare with little fuss. This recipe adds a bit of Chinese flavor, and the mushrooms give it more depth. Reconstituted dried mushrooms could substitute for the fresh for an even deeper, concentrated earthy flavor. Pork or beef could also be used with a slight change in the cooking time.

1 Mix the first six ingredients together and then toss with the chicken, mushrooms, and scallions.

2 Place in a heatproof dish or bowl, cover tightly, and place in a covered steamer. Steam for 35–40 minutes, turn off the steamer, remove the lid, and wait a few minutes before removing the bowl with the chicken. Carefully uncover the bowl and arrange the chicken, mushrooms, and scallions on a serving platter. Pour the juices over the top and garnish with the cilantro, if desired.

CHICKEN HOTPOT
[LAU GA]

2½-pound chicken fryer, cut into 8 or 9 pieces	½ teaspoon salt	1 red or green bell pepper, stemmed, seeded, and cut into 1-inch pieces
3 quarts chicken broth	1 teaspoon whole black peppercorns	1 bunch mustard greens, spinach, Swiss chard, or other greens, washed and large stems removed, then cut into 2-inch-wide strips
2 stalks lemongrass, lightly crushed and cut into 2-inch sections	2 potatoes, or 1 sweet potato, peeled and cut into bite-size pieces	
1 (1-inch) piece ginger, peeled and then sliced into 3 pieces	2 carrots, peeled and cut into bite-size pieces	2–3 serrano or jalapeño chiles, stemmed and sliced
4–5 star anise	6–8 medium mushrooms, halved or quartered	½ medium pineapple, skinned, cored, and cut into bite-size chunks
5 cloves garlic, peeled and lightly smashed	2–3 tomatoes, quartered	8–10 cilantro sprigs
3 tablespoons fish sauce	1 white onion, peeled and cut into 8 wedges	
1 tablespoon rice or distilled white vinegar		

☙ SERVES 4–6 OR MORE AS PART OF A LARGER MEAL ☙

LAU IS THE name for the hotpot dish that is also some-times called a steamboat. It is set in the middle of the table on a charcoal, gas, or electric burner and is filled with flavorful broth; various meats, seafood, vege-tables, and fruits are placed in the almost boiling liq-uid to cook or finish cooking and add their flavors to the broth. Lau refers to the broth used, but the term has become synonymous with the dish. Lau restau-rants are often concentrated in one area, like Phung Hung near the overhead train tracks in old Hanoi, where there are hundreds distinguished by their street numbers only, and alongside Truc Bach Lake. Hotpot is a social event where a number of diners share the same pot and participate in the cooking. Feel free to vary the vegetables listed in this recipe. Lau is often served with some rice to add the broth to, making a soup that finishes the meal. Noodles also make a nice accompaniment to hotpot dishes.

I Rinse the chicken pieces and place in a pot with cool broth. Bring to a boil for 10 minutes, then remove from the heat and skim off any scum that forms on the top.

continued on page 168

2 Return to the heat and add the lemongrass, ginger, star anise, garlic, fish sauce, vinegar, salt, and peppercorns. Cook at a low boil for about 20 minutes. Turn off the heat and let sit for 20 minutes more. Remove the chicken from the pot and cut each piece in half. Strain the broth with a fine strainer or through cheesecloth.

3 Precook the potatoes and carrots in boiling salted water just until done, about 15 minutes; drain and let cool.

4 Place a "lau pot" or other heavy pot in the middle of the table, two-thirds filled with the broth, on top of a heat source sufficient to bring it to a boil.

5 Add some of each of the remaining ingredients along with several pieces of the chicken, being careful not to overfill the pot.

6 After about 10 minutes of cooking in the hotpot, diners may begin to help themselves to the food in the hot broth. Replenish with the additional ingredients as needed. A large spoon or ladle is handy for serving the broth.

CHICKEN, LEMONGRASS, AND CHILE STIR-FRY
[GA XAO XA OT]

1 pound boneless, skinless
  chicken breasts or thighs,
  cut into bite-size chunks
Salt and pepper
2 tablespoons vegetable oil
2 good-size lemongrass stalks,
  thick bottom part only, finely
  minced (about 3 tablespoons)

2–3 red or green serrano or Thai
  chiles, stemmed and chopped
2 teaspoons minced shallots
3 cloves garlic, minced
1 green or red bell pepper, stemmed,
  seeded, and cut into 1-inch chunks

1 medium white onion, peeled
  and cut into 1-inch chunks
1 tablespoon Caramel Sauce (page 40)
2 tablespoons fish sauce or soy sauce
¼ cup chopped cilantro

SERVES 6–8 AS AN APPETIZER OR 4–6 AS PART OF A LARGER MEAL

FOUND IN MANY small restaurants around the country and on the home table, this dish is boldly flavored, and it captures the essence of Vietnamese flavors and a simple cooking method. It can also be made with pork instead of chicken. Usually served as part of an array of dishes, it also works well as the center point of a meal. Another popular way to present this recipe is to serve it along with rice paper wrappers, lettuce leaves, and fresh herbs for each diner to roll up their own wrap to be dipped in sauce.

I Season the chicken with salt and pepper. Heat the oil in a wok and add the lemongrass, chiles, shallots, garlic, bell pepper, and onion; stir-fry for about 30 seconds. Add the chicken and continue stir-frying until it begins to brown, about 2–3 minutes. Add the Caramel Sauce and fish sauce, and stir-fry 1–2 minutes more to coat the chicken with the sauce. Garnish with cilantro and serve.

With over 1,200 miles of coastline and hundreds of rivers and even more lakes and ponds, Vietnam is a treasure of great seafood. Ingredients from the sea are featured in a huge number of Vietnamese recipes, and seafood often makes its way into dishes that center around land-based ingredients too. The Vietnamese are almost fanatical about the freshness of their seafood. Many sea creatures are still alive and swimming moments before they are cooked. Some of the harder-to-come-by seafood items may be available at Asian markets; otherwise, substitution is always an acceptable option. Just make sure that it is as fresh as can be for the best authentic results.

SEAFOOD
DISHES

THE RECIPES

GRILLED FISH HANOI-STYLE WITH RICE NOODLES AND HERBS
[CHA CA HANOI]

MARINADE

2 teaspoons juice from fresh
  galangal or gingerroot, or
  1 teaspoon dried galangal powder
2 teaspoons ground turmeric
1 tablespoon Vietnamese shrimp
  paste, or 2 tablespoons fish sauce
2 teaspoons sugar
3 tablespoons plain yogurt
1 teaspoon rice vinegar

½ teaspoon salt
2 teaspoons vegetable oil

2 pounds catfish, halibut, tilapia, sea
  bass, or other mild yet firm fish fillets
12–16 ounces dried vermicelli
  or other rice noodles
2 tablespoons vegetable oil
½ cup coarsely chopped roasted peanuts
2 cups chopped fresh dill
  tops (1½-inch pieces)

Dash of salt
Handful of chives, or 4 scallions
  (green parts only)
Fresh herbs (Asian basil, mint, cilantro,
  sorrel, Vietnamese coriander, etc.)
Tender lettuce leaves (butter, red
  or green leaf lettuce, etc.)
1 cup Basic Vietnamese Dipping Sauce
  (page 42) with 2 teaspoons sugar added

∞ SERVES 4–6 ∞

THIS DISH IS named after the restaurant in Hanoi that first popularized this method, Cha Ca la Vong. However, I learned this recipe from my friend Khai Binh, the chef of his family's Dzoan Restaurant in Saigon. The original recipe calls for sour rice, a fermented concoction that takes several weeks to prepare, but plain yogurt works well. The classic method of serving this dish is to first grill the fish, then place it in a skillet on a tabletop burner and cook it again with dill and chives or scallions. Here, I recommend you grill or broil the fish in larger pieces and cut them bite-size, then sauté the dill, chives, and peanuts in oil and pour over the fish. Individual portions are then combined in a bowl with rice noodles, fresh herbs, and lettuces by each diner. Cha Ca is usually served along with a sweet dipping sauce and some sliced chiles.

1 Combine all of the marinade ingredients and toss gently with the fish fillets. Set aside for 30 minutes to 1 hour. Grill the fish or broil until done, cut into bite-size pieces, and arrange on a platter; cover to keep warm.

2 Cook the rice noodles until done and then rinse in cool water and set aside.

3 Heat the oil in a skillet or wok and add the peanuts, dill, salt, and chives (cut into 3-inch lengths, then quarter lengthwise). Sauté until fragrant and hot, then pour over the cooked fish pieces. Serve with the noodles, herbs, lettuce, and dipping sauce for each diner to combine on his or her own bowl or plate.

Whenever we settle into a small town or village, having come directly from home, it takes us time to find our feet, to get acclimated, to adjust our expectations for what each individual day will bring. It affects our feelings about the food we eat and how the food tastes.

SHRIMP IN CARAMEL SAUCE
[TOM KHO]

24 ounces medium-to-large shrimp, split and deveined with the shell left on 3 tablespoons Caramel Sauce (page 40)	2 tablespoons fish sauce 2 shallots, or 1 small white onion, peeled and finely chopped 1 clove garlic, minced 1 teaspoon minced ginger (optional)	Dash of salt ½ teaspoon ground black pepper 1 tablespoon vegetable oil 2 scallions, thinly sliced

∞ SERVES 2–3 AS A MAIN DISH OR 4–6 AS PART OF A LARGER MEAL ∞

THIS IS ANOTHER dish that is traditionally cooked in a clay pot, but it may also be prepared in a heavy saucepan or Dutch oven. Slow cooking with the Caramel Sauce and usually only a few other ingredients for flavor coaxes out the most flavor from simple fare. I like the typical unpeeled shrimp for more flavor and texture, but they may be peeled if you prefer. Do not be concerned about overcooking the shrimp; they turn out very nice with an interesting texture and beautiful color, despite the seemingly overlong cooking time. The same method will also work well with firm catfish. Serve with jasmine rice.

1 In a preheated clay pot or heavy saucepan, place the shrimp, Caramel Sauce, fish sauce, shallots, garlic, ginger, salt, and pepper, and bring to a boil. Reduce the heat to just below boiling, give it a good stir, and partially cover the pot. Cook for 8–10 minutes, stirring occasionally. Remove the lid and continue cooking about 5–6 minutes more, adding a little water if needed to prevent burning. (The shrimp should release some juices to keep the sauce fairly moist.) The sauce should be thick and coating the shrimp when done. Remove from the heat and stir in the oil and scallions; serve immediately.

Ingredients from the sea are featured in a huge number of Vietnamese recipes. The Vietnamese are almost fanatical about the freshness of their seafood. Many sea creatures are still alive and swimming moments before they are cooked.

CHARCOAL GRILLED SQUID, SHRIMP, VEGETABLES, AND FRUIT

[MUC VOI TOM NUONG LAC CANH]

MARINADE

3 tablespoons minced shallots

2 teaspoons Chile-Garlic-Oil Table Condiment (page 44), or 3 cloves garlic smashed into a smooth paste with 1–2 serrano or Thai chiles or ½ teaspoon dry chile flakes

⅓ cup finely minced lemongrass

1 tablespoon fish sauce

2 teaspoons soy sauce

2 teaspoons sugar

¼ teaspoon ground black pepper

Dash of salt

2 tablespoons lime juice

3 tablespoons vegetable oil

Tomatoes, onions, jicama, scallions, okra, pineapple, apple, mushrooms, asparagus, long green beans, bell peppers, chiles, and any other vegetables or fruits that you like, cut into sizes appropriate for grilling and manipulating with chopsticks

1–1½ pounds large shrimp, preferably with head and shell on, but peeled may also be used

1–1½ pounds small whole squid (3–5 inches is perfect), cleaned

∽ SERVES 3–4 AS A MAIN DISH OR 6–8 AS PART OF A LARGER MEAL ∽

IN NHA TRANG, the beach resort and fishing community on the southeastern coast of Vietnam, fresh seafood is everywhere. To enjoy the abundant harvest from the sea, you need go no farther than the beach, where ladies are bearing don gang—the clever setup of a bamboo pole hoisted over the shoulder with two baskets suspended on each end. One basket is full of fresh fish, prawns, lobster, squid, and a myriad of other delicacies, and the other holds a charcoal grill. They will be happy to prepare your selection on the spot. Tourists and locals alike also flock to the Lac Canh restaurant, where you can also order fresh seafood and an array of marinated meats and vegetables to be cooked by you on the clay brazier filled with glowing charcoal embers and brought to your table.

The aroma of the sizzling delights combined with the blue smoke in the air and the clink of ice cubes in the beer glasses is intoxicating. This recipe, using prawns and squid, is inspired by that experience; however, feel free to choose any seafood that you fancy—the fresher the better. If you are not set up for the grill-your-own style of serving, you can always grill the seafood and vegetables ahead of time and serve them on a platter. Serve with limes and dipping sauces.

I Mix all of the marinade ingredients together well and let sit for a few minutes to allow the flavors to

continued on page 184

blend. Remove one-third of the marinade and toss with the vegetables and fruit.

2 Combine the remaining marinade with the shrimp and squid, and marinate for 20–30 minutes.

NOTE: If using shell-on shrimp, trim the legs and antenna with scissors to prevent burning (you may also split and devein the shrimp to allow more of the marinade flavor to penetrate).

3 Preheat a charcoal or gas grill to medium high. Grill the seafood, vegetables, and fruits in batches. Your guests should begin eating as soon as the first items are ready, and the cooking duties may rotate as everyone enjoys the results.

GRILLED FISH FILLETS WITH GINGER SAUCE
[CA NUONG NUOC XOT GUNG]

24 ounces fresh fish fillets (snapper, halibut, sea bass, tuna, etc.), cut into 4 portions
¼ cup lime juice
Salt and pepper
2 tablespoons chopped fresh dill leaves
2 tablespoons vegetable oil, divided

1 (1-inch) piece ginger, peeled and cut into 3 smaller slices
1 tablespoon minced shallot
1–2 red serrano or Thai chiles, stemmed and thinly sliced
2 stalks lemongrass, thinly sliced
2 tablespoons fish or soy sauce
2 teaspoons sugar

½ cup rice wine or dry sherry
2 tablespoons rice wine or distilled white vinegar
2 scallions, thinly sliced into rings
⅛ cup cool chicken broth or water mixed with 2 teaspoons cornstarch
1 tablespoon sesame oil
2 tablespoons finely julienned ginger

∞ SERVES 4 ∞

A SOMEWHAT CONTEMPORARY dish combining Vietnamese and Chinese flavors, the grilled fish could also be prepared by pan-searing. For a more dramatic presentation, use a whole fish and portion it at the table. This could also be part of a large feast with many dishes. As with all Vietnamese cooking, the freshness of the fish is the most important secret to the success of this recipe. Serve with steamed rice, stir-fried vegetables, and a salad.

I Coat the fish fillets with the lime juice, season with salt and pepper, and spread the dill leaves over the entire surface, pressing a bit to keep them in place. Cover and refrigerate for 1–2 hours.

2 Remove the fish from the refrigerator and preheat a grill.

3 In a wok, heat 1 tablespoon vegetable oil and sauté the ginger, shallot, chiles, and lemongrass for 30 seconds. Add the fish sauce and sugar followed by the wine and vinegar. Boil for 1 minute; add the scallions and the broth/cornstarch mixture. Simmer for 5 minutes and turn off the heat. Remove the ginger slices.

4 Mix together the sesame oil and remaining vegetable oil, and brush it over all surfaces of the fish. Grill on medium-high heat about 4–5 minutes on the first side, depending on the thickness of the fillets. Turn over and cook just until done. Place on a serving platter, pour the sauce over top, and garnish with ginger.

SQUID, LEMONGRASS, AND CHILE STIR-FRY WITH COCONUT MILK
[MUC XAO XA NUOC COT DUA]

1 pound whole squid, cleaned
Salt and pepper
2 tablespoons vegetable oil

2 good-size lemongrass stalks, thick bottom part only, finely minced (about 3 tablespoons)

2 teaspoons Vietnamese yellow curry powder or Madras curry powder
1–2 red or green serrano or Thai chiles, stemmed and chopped
2 teaspoons minced shallot
3 cloves garlic, minced
1 teaspoon sugar

1 green or red bell pepper, stemmed, seeded, and cut into 1-inch chunks
1 medium white onion, peeled and cut into 1-inch chunks
2 tablespoons fish sauce
½ cup unsweetened coconut milk
¼ cup chopped cilantro

☞ SERVES 2–3 AS A MAIN DISH OR 4–6 AS PART OF A LARGER MEAL ☜

ALMOST A CURRY but cooked for a shorter period of time, this spicy dish is often prepared using eel. I have also seen it made using some chunks of fresh pineapple to add sweetness as a foil for the chile heat. Serve it with rice and a salad or steamed vegetables.

1 Season the squid with salt and pepper; set aside. Heat the oil in a wok. Sear the squid briefly in the hot oil; remove and reserve.

2 Add the lemongrass, curry powder, chiles, shallot, garlic, sugar, bell pepper, and onion to the hot oil, and stir-fry for about 30 seconds. Add the fish sauce and coconut milk, bring to a boil, reduce to a low boil, and cook for 8–10 minutes, or until the mixture has thickened.

3 Slice the squid into ¼-inch rings and add to the wok. Cook for 1–2 minutes more while stirring. When heated through, garnish with the cilantro and serve.

BATTERED PRAWNS WRAPPED IN LETTUCE WITH HERBS
[TOM CHIEN BOT MI TRUNG]

2 eggs, well beaten
1 1/2 cups cold water
1 1/2 cups rice flour, divided
1/2 teaspoon salt
1/2 teaspoon ground black pepper
16–18 large prawns or shrimp
 (about 1 1/2 pounds)

2 cups vegetable oil
16–18 lettuce leaves (butter,
 red leaf, or romaine)
1 1/2 cups bean sprouts
1 medium cucumber, sliced
Fresh herbs (Asian basil, cilantro,
 fish mint, mint, red perilla,
 Vietnamese coriander, etc.)

Basic Vietnamese Dipping Sauce
 (page 42), Soy-Lime Dipping Sauce
 (page 32), Salt, Pepper, and Lime
 Dipping Sauce (page 33), Sweet
 Chile Sauce (page 34), or others
 as desired

☜ SERVES 3–4 AS A MAIN DISH OR 6–8 AS AN APPETIZER ☞

PERFECTLY CRISPY, NOT greasy, battered prawns along with the crunch of vegetables and the aroma of herbs, highlighted by salty and spicy dipping sauces—these wraps will send you into near ecstasy. Hot oil is the secret to non-greasy fried food. Extensive testing has proven that ice-cold beer is the perfect accompaniment to these prawns.

1 Mix together the eggs, water, 1 cup flour, salt, and pepper to make a smooth batter. Add more water as needed to create a light pancake-batter consistency.

2 Soak the prawns in very cold salted water for 2–3 minutes and drain well.

3 Heat the oil in a wok until just a few wisps of smoke rise from the surface (about 365 degrees). First dredge each prawn in the remaining flour, dip in the batter, and gently lay in the hot oil. Cook, a few at a time, turning occasionally until the batter is a deep golden brown. Remove from the oil, drain, and place on paper towels.

4 Serve on a platter with the lettuce, vegetables, and herbs with bowls of dipping sauces. Provide a plate for each diner to make his or her own wrap.

SOFT-SHELLED CRAB WITH CHILES AND LEMONGRASS

[CUA OT XA]

1½ cups rice flour	⅓ cup finely minced lemongrass	2 teaspoons sugar
½ teaspoon salt	2 tablespoons minced garlic	2 tablespoons fish sauce
¼ teaspoon ground black pepper	2 tablespoons minced shallot	½ cup fish stock, chicken
⅓ cup vegetable oil	1–2 red serrano or Thai chiles,	stock, or water
1¾–2 pounds live (or frozen and	minced, or 2 teaspoons	2 scallions, sliced into thin rings
thawed) soft-shell crabs	crushed red chile paste, or	¼ cup cilantro leaves
2 eggs, well beaten	½ teaspoon dry red chile flakes	

∽ SERVES 4–6 AS AN APPETIZER OR AS PART OF A LARGER MEAL ∽

I LEARNED THIS method from my new chef friend Khai on my first trip to Vietnam. We used the crabs in a salad of mangosteen fruit that was a delicious pairing of the rich and spicy hot flavors of the crab against the creamy, sweet, and sour flavors of that fruit. These crabs could be used as an appetizer just as they are, as part of a salad as Khai and I did, or as a main course dish as part of a larger meal. Precooked hard-shell crab of any size could be substituted for the soft-shell ones. Simply skip the first step of cooking the crab, crack the shells slightly to allow the flavors to penetrate, and then heat the crab with the sauce after it has been fried.

1 Combine the flour, salt, and pepper; set aside.

2 Heat the oil in a wok. Toss the crabs in the eggs, then dredge in the flour mixture and place in the oil a few at a time. Cook until golden brown and then drain on paper towels. When all of the crabs have been browned, pour off all but 2 tablespoons of the oil.

3 To the hot oil add the lemongrass, garlic, and shallot; stir-fry for 30 seconds. Add the chiles and sugar, stir for a moment, and then add the fish sauce and stock.

4 Boil the sauce for a few seconds, add the scallions, and then return the crabs to the wok. Toss crabs in the sauce until well coated and warmed through. Place on a serving plate and garnish with cilantro.

Rice is the lifeblood of Vietnamese eating. It's seen at almost every meal, and without it, food is considered merely a snack—rice makes it a meal and rice alone still constitutes eating a meal. It has a number of varieties in both the long-grain and short-grain versions, and the quality levels, although subtle in many cases, are carefully noticed by discerning Vietnamese cooks. Rice is also made into noodles, cakes, and papers for wrapping food.

RICE & BANH DISHES

THE RECIPES

FRAGRANT STEAMED JASMINE RICE
[COM]

3¼ cups water
2 cups jasmine rice

❧ SERVES 4–6 AS A SIDE DISH ☙

AN ESSENTIAL PART of the Vietnamese diet, rice is revered and cooked with care. A typical question from a Vietnamese is "have you had rice?" meaning have you eaten? There are many grades, sizes, and qualities of rice—use the best you can find. Rinsing the rice prevents starchiness and makes it more fragrant. Rice may be cooked in a rice cooker or a lidded pot. Vietnamese cooks do not add salt to the rice while it is cooking. This recipe is for a lidded pot; follow the directions on your rice cooker if you use that method.

1 Rinse the rice in cool water until it runs clear; drain thoroughly.

2 Place the water in a lidded pot along with the rinsed rice and bring to a boil. Cover and boil for 1 minute; then reduce the heat to very low and cook for 15 minutes more. Turn off the heat and leave covered for 5–10 minutes before serving. Fluff with chopsticks or a fork.

SHRIMP AND CHICKEN FRIED RICE

[COM CHIEN TOM GA]

3 (2-inch) sections lemongrass, or 3 slices peeled ginger, slightly smashed, divided

2 teaspoons + 1 tablespoon fish or soy sauce

2 teaspoons sugar, divided

10 ounces skinless chicken thigh or breast meat, cut into bite-size pieces (you may also use leftover, grilled, roasted, or steamed chicken meat)

3 tablespoons vegetable oil, divided

12 ounces small-to-medium shrimp, peeled and deveined

1 clove garlic, peeled and lightly smashed

1 medium carrot, peeled and sliced diagonally

1 1/2 cups bite-size broccoli florets

1/2 cup sliced fresh mushrooms

1/2 red bell pepper, seeded and diced into 3/4-inch pieces

1–2 tablespoons fish sauce

1 teaspoon chile paste (optional)

2 tablespoons rice wine or dry sherry

2 scallions, sliced diagonally into 1/2-inch sections

2 1/2 cups cold cooked rice

1/4 cup chopped cilantro

∽ SERVES 3–4 AS A MAIN DISH ∾

VIETNAMESE FRIED RICE is much lighter than traditional Chinese style; it uses much less oil and is only lightly sauced. The possible combinations of additions to the rice are limitless, from just a vegetable or two and some aromatics to several kinds of meat, eggs, seafood, and vegetables. It is also a great outlet for leftover grilled and stir-fried meats. Use your best judgment, based on ingredients and size of pieces, as to what order you add them to the wok and cooking time to ensure that everything is done and nothing is overcooked.

I Mince 1 stalk lemongrass or 1 slice ginger and combine with 2 teaspoons fish sauce, 1 teaspoon sugar, and the chicken. **NOTE:** If using cooked chicken, omit this step and the marinade ingredients.

2 Heat 2 tablespoons oil in a wok. Add the chicken and stir-fry for 2 minutes, add the shrimp and continue cooking until the chicken is just done. Remove from the wok and reserve.

3 Heat the remaining oil in the wok, add the garlic and remaining lemongrass or ginger and fry for about 15 seconds. Add the carrot and broccoli, stir-frying for 2–3 minutes. Add the mushrooms and bell pepper, and cook 2 minutes more. Remove the lemongrass and garlic, add the fish sauce, chile paste, remaining sugar, wine, and scallions to the vegetables; heat briefly and add the chicken and shrimp back to the pan. When everything is hot, add the rice and stir-fry until heated through. Serve garnished with the cilantro sprinkled over top.

THE PEOPLE
AND FLAVORS OF
THE NORTH

An overnight train ride from Hanoi northwest to Lao Cai, near the Chinese border, will put you in the heart of the ethnic minority hill tribe groups. About an hour and a half drive, sometimes hair-raising at times, over the mountains and hills to the northwest will take you to Bac Ha. Every Sunday morning the roads and trails through the hills surrounding Bac Ha are teeming with ethnic minority people from the neighboring villages and countryside, heading to the weekly market. This is one of the most colorful markets to be found anywhere. Each minority group—Black Hmong, Flower Hmong, Tay, Red Dao, Thai, White Thai, and many more—are clad in their own brightly colored, unique, hand-woven, dyed and sewn outfits that immediately identify their membership in the respective groups. This

market, while entertaining some tourists, is largely focused on the local trade, and everything—including food staples, fruits and vegetables, freshly killed meats, seafood, poultry, live animals, farming implements, cloth, yarn, dyes, clothing, footwear, tobacco, rice and corn wine, and just about anything else that you could imagine—is being bought, sold, and bartered for here. Numerous languages are spoken, with Vietnamese being the common language for the market, although it is the second or third dialect for most of the participants. Food vendors encircle the main market, and anything from Pho and other various noodle soups to horse stew and a medley of offal and organ meats seasoned with wild local herbs and chiles can be found and eaten here on roughly hewn low-set wooden tables and benches. The Bac Ha market is an unforgettable experience for an outsider.

SIZZLING CRÊPES

[BANH XEO]

BATTER

2¼ cups rice flour

2½ cups water

½ cup coconut milk (unsweetened, fresh, or canned)

1 teaspoon salt

1 teaspoon ground turmeric

½ teaspoon yellow curry powder (optional)

2 scallions, very thinly sliced

FILLING

⅓ to ½ cup vegetable oil

½ pound pork shoulder or country-style boneless ribs, thinly sliced, or ½ pound ground pork

½ pound small or medium shrimp (peeled and deveined or left in shells with only the legs and tails trimmed)

½ cup thinly sliced onion

4 ounces sliced fresh mushrooms such as shiitake, brown crimini, oyster, white button, etc. (optional)

4 cups fresh bean sprouts

GARNISH AND CONDIMENT

16–24 lettuce or mustard greens leaves

Fresh herbs (cilantro, Thai basil, red perilla, mint, Vietnamese mint, sorrel, etc.)

Thinly sliced, peeled, and seeded cucumber (optional)

1 cup or more Basic Vietnamese Dipping Sauce (page 42)

☜ SERVES 4–6 AS A MAIN DISH OR 8–10 AS AN APPETIZER ☞

THERE ARE MANY versions of these omelet-like rice flour crêpes that are named for the sound that they make as they sizzle on the hot skillet. In the center of the country around Hue, where they probably originated, and farther south in Nha Trang, they are called Banh Khoai (delightful crêpes). They are small-ish, around 5–7 inches in diameter. In Saigon, they are enormous, 12 inches or more across. In the central and northern regions, a simple rice flour batter is used; however, in the south, coconut milk is added for additional richness and crispiness. The traditional filling, described here, is pork and shrimp along with bean sprouts and sometimes sliced mushrooms too, but you could use just about anything you like: sliced chicken, tofu, cooked eggs, various vegetables, etc. After cooking, the crêpes are broken into smaller pieces, wrapped in lettuce with fresh herbs, and then dipped in various sauces.

1 Vigorously whisk all the batter ingredients except the scallions in a bowl until smooth. Stir in the scallions and set aside for at least 20–30 minutes.

2 Heat an 8- to 12-inch nonstick or well-seasoned cast-iron skillet on high and add a generous amount of oil to coat the pan. Add ⅛ to ¼ of the total pork, shrimp, onion, and mushrooms, depending on how many crêpes you plan to make. Stir gently while cooking for 30–45 seconds, or until starting to color and the onions can be smelled.

3 Stir the batter well and add ¼–⅓ cup to the same pan; swirl around to coat evenly (you want a thin coating). Add about ¾–1 cup of the bean sprouts and spread over half of the crêpe. Lower the heat to medium, cover the pan until the bean sprouts have begun to soften, about 3 minutes or so. Uncover and cook another 3–5 minutes, or until the bottom of the crêpe is crispy and golden brown. Lift one side with a spatula and gently fold in half. Serve on a platter with the lettuce, herbs, cucumber, and dipping sauces, or on individual plates or bowls for each diner to assemble his or her wraps.

NOTE: You may want to cut the crêpes into serving pieces, or let your guests do it themselves for extra entertainment.

Vegetables play a significant role in the Vietnamese kitchen and on the table. They lend color, flavor, and texture to a recipe and provide essential nutrients to the people who eat them. Sometimes they are the centerpiece of a dish, and other times they are a supporting cast member. Once again, freshness plays a vital role. It is better to select an alternative or forego the vegetable altogether if it means using one that is less than optimally fresh.

VEGETABLE DISHES

THE RECIPES

TOFU AND SPINACH STIR-FRY
[RAU MUONG XAO DAU PHU]

8 ounces firm tofu, drained and cut into ½-inch cubes	3–4 cloves garlic, thinly sliced	fish sauce (optional)
3 tablespoons vegetable oil, divided	Sliced Thai, serrano, or jalapeño chiles	1½ pounds fresh spinach leaves (about 2 bunches), washed
1 (⅛-inch-thick) ginger slice, gently smashed with the side of a knife	1 teaspoon chopped shallot (optional)	and stem ends trimmed
	1 tablespoon soy sauce	½ teaspoon sugar
	1 teaspoon oyster sauce or	

∽ SERVES 2–3 AS A MAIN DISH OR 4–6 AS PART OF A LARGER MEAL ∽

WATER SPINACH (RAU muong), a green that is often mislabeled in English as morning glory, is easy to come by in Vietnam. You will find it served on many a table. In the U.S., I usually substitute regular spinach or any of the other available greens with excellent results. Adding tofu to this common side dish adds another component of texture and color, and also makes it a dish that could serve as a vegetarian main course.

1 Sear the tofu slices in a wok or heavy skillet in 2 tablespoons oil until they show a little color around the edges. Remove from the pan, drain on paper towels, and reserve. Heat the remaining oil until very hot. Add the ginger, garlic, chiles, and shallot; stir-fry until fragrant.

2 Add the soy sauce, oyster sauce, and spinach. Stir-fry for 1–2 minutes; add the sugar and reserved tofu. Cook a few seconds more, tossing well, until the tofu is heated through. Serve immediately.

PUMPKIN IN COCONUT MILK
[BI DO HAM DUA]

1½ cups unsweetened coconut
  milk, or 1 (13-ounce) can
¾ cup water
1½ teaspoons sugar
½ teaspoon salt

½ teaspoon dry turmeric
2 teaspoons fish or soy sauce
1 (1-inch) piece ginger, peeled
  and cut into 3 slices
½ medium white onion,
  peeled and thinly sliced

1 (1½–2-pound) pumpkin, skin
  and seeds removed, then
  cut into 1-inch chunks
2 tablespoons chopped cilantro
  or Vietnamese coriander

☙ SERVES 4–6 AS PART OF A LARGER MEAL ☙

A SIMPLE BUT striking dish from the south, where coconuts abound, the colors are vibrant and the flavor is rich and exotic. Traditionally prepared with the greenish-skinned cooking pumpkins seen at the markets around the area, and sometimes with sweet potatoes added as well, they can be substituted with acorn or butternut squash. This dish is usually served as a side dish at a meal containing a variety of selections. Be careful not to overcook the pumpkin—you want it tender, but it will disintegrate if cooked too long past that stage.

1 In a saucepan, mix the coconut milk and water; add the sugar, salt, turmeric, and fish sauce; stir well to combine. Add the ginger, onion, and pumpkin, and bring to a low boil; stir gently and reduce the heat to simmer.

2 Cook for about 20–25 minutes, stirring occasionally. Check to see if the pumpkin is tender and cook a few more minutes or as needed (add a bit more water if the sauce gets too dry). Remove from the heat, remove the ginger, and let sit a few minutes to thicken the sauce. Garnish with cilantro and serve.

The food in the north tends to be a bit more austere than its southern counterpart, utilizing a simpler array of seasonings and a more conservative approach, but flavor and sophistication are not lacking by any means.

STIR-FRIED GREEN BEANS WITH CHILES

[DAU DUA XAO OT]

1 pound long beans or other green beans, ends trimmed, cut into sections or left whole 2 tablespoons vegetable oil	2 medium shallots, peeled and sliced into ⅛-inch-thick rings 1 or 2 red jalapeño, serrano, Fresno, or Thai chiles, stemmed and cut into ⅛-inch slices	1 teaspoon sugar 1 tablespoon fish or soy sauce 1 teaspoon hoisin or oyster sauce 2 tablespoons water

∞ SERVES 4–6 AS PART OF A LARGER MEAL ∞

ONE OF THE things that surprised me about the food when I first came to Vietnam was how often I was served green beans in private homes and at restaurants. They came steamed, stir-fried, almost plain, and with a myriad of different seasonings. It may have been the peak season for beans, but they are probably available year-round, and their ease of preparation and ability to pair with a wide variety of dishes makes them popular. For the photo of this recipe, I used Chinese long beans, sometimes called chopstick beans in Vietnam, but any green bean or even sugar snap peas could be used. I have chosen to spice the dish up with chiles, but you may elect to keep it milder and allow your guests to add the chiles as they like.

I Blanch the beans in boiling salted water for about 2 minutes; immediately immerse into ice water to stop the cooking process and to set the color; drain well.

2 Heat the oil to the point of just smoking and add the shallots and chiles, followed by the beans. Stir-fry for about 2–3 minutes, or until the beans and shallots have a little dark color around the edges.

3 Add the sugar and fish sauce, and stir for about 15 seconds. Add the hoisin and water, and stir again to mix. Bring the water to a boil briefly, stir again, and remove the beans from the wok to a serving plate.

Steamed Vegetables
[Rau Hap]

1 or more vegetables (see introduction
  and feel free to add), washed
  and cut into bite-size pieces

SERVES ANY NUMBER

TO GO WITH a meal consisting of rich and/or spicy dishes, sometimes simple and plain, steamed or boiled vegetables are what is needed. On the home table in Vietnam, steamed vegetables make a frequent appearance. Steaming maintains the bright color of fresh vegetables and preserves the nutritional content. The method works with a wide selection of vegetables, from carrots, kohlrabi, broccoli, cauliflower, sweet potatoes, and asparagus, to beans, bok choy, cabbage, and a whole slew of different vines and greens. The cooking times will vary based upon the vegetable used and how large the pieces are. You will learn the timing through experience. There is no need to season them, as they will be dipped in the table sauces or combined with boldly flavored dishes.

I Set up a steamer (stacking Asian bamboo steamers work very well, but any number of commercial or improvised setups will work fine). Heat the water in the steamer to boiling (make sure that there is enough to complete the cooking without needing to add more). Place the vegetables in the steamer on a rack or basket that keeps them above the boiling water; cover and steam. Carefully check vegetables periodically to ensure that they do not overcook. When done, remove from the steamer and serve immediately.

Stir-Fried Bitter Greens
[Cai Tau Xao]

3 tablespoons vegetable oil 3 cloves garlic, sliced	1 pound bitter greens, washed and any large, tough stems removed Dash of salt	¼ teaspoon ground black pepper 2 tablespoons oyster or soy sauce

∽ SERVES 4–6 AS PART OF A LARGER MEAL ∽

THE SHARPLY FLAVORED taste of mustard greens, chard, kale, beet tops, and other bitter greens with a touch of garlic adds a simple contrast to rich, sweet, or spicy hot dishes. Other less bitter greens like water spinach, bok choy, Chinese broccoli, cabbage, and regular spinach may be used in this recipe too.

1 Heat the oil in a wok on high until it is just smoking. Add the garlic and greens, then toss quickly to prevent burning; keep stirring for about 1 minute.

2 Add the salt, pepper, and oyster sauce; stir, cover, and cook until the greens are ready, about 1½–2 minutes (they should still be a bit crunchy). Serve immediately.

SOURCES

Asian markets and, to some extent, Latin American, Caribbean, and Middle Eastern markets are your best source for supplies of fresh and dry goods. Many farmers markets also carry some fresh herbs, fruits, and vegetables that are called for in Vietnamese cookery. Mainstream supermarkets are often a good source of Asian ingredients, and many of the fresh items needed are becoming more commonly available. Mail order and online stores are a valuable resource for hard-to-find items or if you do not live near any of the resources mentioned above.

GENERAL INGREDIENTS AND PRODUCE

ORIENTAL PANTRY
423 Great Road
Acton, MA 01720-4120
(978) 264-4576

PACIFIC RIM GOURMET
16417 Sherman Street
Volente, TX 78641
www.pacificrimgourmet.com

MELISSA'S WORLD VARIETY PRODUCE, INC.
PO Box 21127
Los Angeles, CA 90021
(800) 588-0151
www.melissas.com

EQUIPMENT AND TABLEWARE

UTAWA-NO-YAKATA
96 Linwood Plaza #358
Fort Lee, NJ 07024
(800) 269-5099

TAJIMI USA INC.
Attn: MOD
240 South Main Street, Ste K
S. Hackensack, NJ 07606
www.utsuwa.com

THE WOK SHOP
718 Grant Avenue
San Francisco, CA 94108
(415) 989-3797
www.wokshop.com

SEED SOURCES

SANDY MUSH HERBS NURSERY
316 Surrett Cove Road
Leicester, NC 28748
(828) 683-2014
www.sandymushherbs.com
Ships live herbs, lemongrass, etc.

KITAZAWA SEED COMPANY
P.O. Box 13220
Oakland, CA 94661-3220
(510) 595-1188
www.kitazawaseed.com

RICHTERS HERBS
357 Highway 47
Goodwood, ON L0C 1A0
Canada
(905) 640-6677
www.richters.com

INDOOR HERB GARDENS

I just completed testing of the AeroGarden indoor growing system, and I am amazed at how well it works. They have a selection of seed kits (I tested the basil variety) that grow herbs, tomatoes, chiles, strawberries, and lettuce in your kitchen. It grows things quickly and can't be beat for freshness. It is especially nice during the winter months when your garden is fallow and the farmers markets have very little fresh produce.

www.aerogrow.com

INDEX

METRIC CONVERSION CHART

VOLUME MEASUREMENTS		WEIGHT MEASUREMENTS		TEMPERATURE CONVERSION	
U.S.	Metric	U.S.	Metric	Fahrenheit	Celsius
1 teaspoon	5 ml	½ ounce	15 g	250	120
1 tablespoon	15 ml	1 ounce	30 g	300	150
¼ cup	60 ml	3 ounces	90 g	325	160
⅓ cup	75 ml	4 ounces	115 g	350	180
½ cup	125 ml	8 ounces	225 g	375	190
⅔ cup	150 ml	12 ounces	350 g	400	200
¾ cup	175 ml	1 pound	450 g	425	220
1 cup	250 ml	2¼ pounds	1 kg	450	230